KARMA, REINCARNATION & OUR MORAL COMPASS

MOTILAL BANARSIDASS INTERNATIONAL
• DELHI •

KARMA,
REINCARNATION
&
OUR MORAL
COMPASS

Ethics & Value in the
Evolution of Oneness

ROBERT SACHS

MOTILAL BANARSIDASS
INTERNATIONAL
DELHI

First Indian Edition : Delhi, 2022

ISBN : 978-93-92510-11-3

Also available at
MOTILAL BANARSIDASS INTERNATIONAL
41 U.A. Bungalow Road, (Back Lane)Jawahar Nagar, Delhi - 110 007
#4361 (basement) Lane #3,Ansari Road, Darya Ganj, New Delhi - 110002
203 Royapettah High Road, Mylapore, Chennai - 600 004
Samar Auddy 56/2, Ahiritola Street, Kolkata - 700 005
Stockist : Motilal Books Ashok Rajpath, Near Kali Mandir, Patna - 800004

Printed & Bound by
MOTILAL BANARSIDASS INTERNATIONAL

Praise for *The Ecology of Oneness...*

"I am glad that my friend of many years, Bob Sachs, has again written a book which brings together practical and important steps on the way to the realization of different transcendent cultures. Like much of his former work it exemplifies methods to see clearly and avoid wasting precious time while choosing one's spiritual path. Myself, I enjoy his observations concerning Diamond Way Buddhism and wish both him and his readers a period of rich discoveries. May many have benefit!"

Lama Ole Nydahl
author of *The Way Things Are, Buddha and Love,* and *Fearless Death*

"Robert Sachs's new book *The Ecology of Oneness* explores the relationship of the spiritual experience and perceptions to our relationship to the world. In the first section of the book, he shares his personal experiences and family story, then moves onto the larger picture with a strong encouragement to see life from a greater perspective than our everyday minds.
The author offers a broad sweep of life on the origins of life on Earth, its relationship to the vastness of the cosmos, while reminding readers of our inter-connection and inter-dependence with it all. He reminds us of how our long biological history continues to influence our present. From this macro and micro perspective, he draws on the insights of the wisdom traditions of the East, science and philosophy to offer a synthesis of a worldview. His book shows the ethics and value of an exploration of Oneness, both theoretical and experiential.
Robert Sachs highlights the importance of Oneness with its explicit importance in terms of the ecological realities. Writing as an American with a variety of religious and cultural influences, Robert Sachs offers a strong critique of the harmful impacts of consumerism and the desire for more and more updated goods. He points to a different set of priorities.
The Ecology of Oneness book makes a valuable contribution to the exploration of our relationship to each other, to the world and to the universe."

Christopher Titmus, Buddhist teacher
author of *An Awakened Life*

'A powerful book full of provocative insights'
Tim Freke, author of *Lucid Living* and *How Long is Now?*

"The honesty, humility, wit, and wisdom Robert Sachs exudes in *The Ecology of Oneness: Awakening in a Free World* is the greatest demonstration of how the unconditional peace and love that our world yearns for can become the reality we live. With his many years involved with numerous wisdom traditions, no one is more worthy of delivering this very timely yet timeless book. Sachs grounds our spiritual pride and urges us to step out of the intellectual wisdom in our heads. He says enough with the spiritual clichés and concepts, it's time to make a choice and let our spirituality be known through the life we live. Skillfully wise with extreme humor, this book leads us into a tribeless land where boundaries dissolve and compassion is king. It implores us to move into this land with fierce courage and an open mind, so that we can reside in the oneness of this land as it is at the root of our hearts."

Jason Gregory
author of The Science and Practice of Humility...

"The real deal! Robert Sachs, *The Ecology of Oneness*, offers a compelling model of consciousness and the role it's playing in the creative evolution for a thriving world. Through a beautiful synthesis of ancient insight and wisdom with modern science, Robert gives our mind a reason to accept what our heart already knows -- that love is the great healer of life, and the power to love into wholeness lives within each of us. This is so much more than a good read . . . it's a portal of truth!"

Dr. Darren R. Weissman
Best Selling Author and Developer of The LifeLine Technique

"The inspirational teachings of Bob Sachs have enhanced our lives. Bob speaks from such a pure and sincere place, with love, gentleness, wisdom, and great humility."

Deva Premal and Miten
singers, songwrtiters, and renown mantra performers

"Robert Sachs has written a fascinating book that brings together esoteric wisdom of the world's faiths with the discoveries of modern neuroscience and brain plasticity. Provocative and even irreverent at times, Sachs is always sensitive to the nuances of the human condition for facilitating practical health and wellbeing. His new popular book, The Ecology of Oneness, provides a broad vision of how we all can move forward together to create a compassionate foundation for a building a more inclusive free world for ourselves and our children."

Drs. Ernest and Kathryn Rossi
Founding Editors, The International Journal of Psychosocial Genomics;
Consciousness & Health Research
Author (Dr. Ernest) of *The Psychobiology of Gene Expression*

Dedication

A wise man from the East once told me that on the rough seas of the spiritual journey, a good teacher was one who rowed you to the shores of your destiny, then burned your boat. The return home was your job.

Over the years I have shared this story in books and lectures, thinking that I understood the lesson imparted; that in the process of us completing the journey, of going to other shore or proverbial "mountain" for whatever message we thought we were looking for and returning home with wisdom gleaned, perhaps to enjoy a hero's welcome, the teacher would be with you until it was time to return. It was then for you to reach deep within yourself to figure out how to get back. And more than likely, you would be forever changed and it was quite questionable whether a hero's welcome would be what your new being would arrive back to. This last bit of wisdom of what the return would be like was imparted to me by another man from the East who said that once you embrace the Dharma, the Sanskrit term to mean the "truth" or "way things are," you would be treated lower than a dog in the street.

From study, but especially through the many twists and turns in my life's and experiences, I grew to understand from looking at traditions both East and West, that completing the journey is a process of individuation; coming to know for oneself beyond what one has studied in books, texts, and liturgical prayer, making it all real, authentic. The hero's journey, the path of the ascetic, the trials, tests, and tribulations of believers and faithful. In the West, the spiritual classic, *The Cloud of Unknowing*, tells how in the final steps to knowing God, one reaches through a cloud, not seeing where you are going, not knowing what exactly one will find beyond the cloud, but also knowing that there is really no point in turning back.

I repeated the stories and shared my insights with others in a rather "off-the-cuff" manner with what, I must admit, was an unknowing pride of someone truly not tested. I did not really 'know" until, as a Buddhist student, my beloved teacher of many years masterfully rowed me to the other shore and burned my boat. In a crowded meditation hall, I approached him for a blessing and words of guidance. Uncharacteristically he reached out and took my hand, smiled lovingly at me and told me that I should not come to see him anymore. He told me I had an unusual mind. I asked him what I should do with this unusual mind of mine. And, as the wisest and most clairvoyant man I have ever met, he said, "I have no idea."

And, I have never felt freer. There are times when I feel lost, but I have become a lot more discerning about what I need and don't need for the final steps of my journey.

Thus, with tremendous love and gratitude I thank him for the gift of a burnt boat and the opportunity to share what I am about to share in this book.

For, I am not writing this book as a Buddhist, although the spiritual discipline of my adult years originates primarily from the Tibetan Buddhist tradition I have been immersed in for close to forty years. Rather, I am writing this book as an American who is the product of different cultures, races, religions, and social influences in a time of great global turbulence at both the micro and macro levels.

Stepping out of the security of a parochial perspective, I am more firmly convinced in Teilhard de Chardin's oft quoted "We are not human beings having a spiritual experience, but rather spiritual beings having a human experience." Thus every bit of life is a spiritual journey. Everyone is our teacher. Each one of us is on a boat trying to get to the other shore, trying to wake up to our sense of wholeness.

The problem is that our boats are in dangerous waters. In a world where traditions collide and the absolutes we thought we could rely on as the safety nets are torn asunder, what we thought we could rely on – political, religious, cultural, interpersonal, and environmental concepts and realities - have become so evidently shaken, that we are being called upon like never before to "get real;" to wake up both personally and collectively.

The Tibetans say that a Dark Age is not a predictable time period, but rather the aggregation of confusion that creates clouds that conceal light.

Thus it is that in the shroud of cloud, we must awaken. We must develop the discipline of mindfulness, find and cultivate courage, and endure as we create for ourselves and others a possible, sustainable future. There are many who want to paint pictures of gloom and doom. This is not helpful. But neither are Pollyanna utopian promises. For, if we hold on to the gloom and doom, we'll never try and our strengths will go untested. But worse still, if our utopian vision does not come to be, we'll lose our courage, become despondent, perhaps give up, and the will to try again may not be that easy to rekindle.

Somewhere between hell and Disneyland is where we are, stuck in the clouds not knowing.

And whether we recognize them or not, we have tools and we have abilities. At the most basic level, we love life and see that that which makes us happiest is loving others and seeing them happy as well. This is the altruistic mindset of an Ecology of Oneness. Although selfishness is very much on parade in the avarice and greed we see cannibalizing our world, even the most closed heart knows in its inner recesses that acting from an Ecology of Oneness perspective is both our personal and collective salvation.

If we consciously or even unconsciously recognize this as true, then we are not lost. We can continue our journey.

It's time to get to work.

As a parting note before we enter into the collective journey of "Awakening in a Free World" as I envision it, I want you to know that I am not writing this book as "the truth" for you to buy into. I am sharing as honestly as I can the truths that I have learned and attempted to practice. For, other than the truly enlightened amongst us and through history who can purely impart truth, I believe the best the rest of us can do is to be and share with honesty. In that we remain heartfelt and vulnerable to each other and open to what lies before us.

As we are all teachers and mentors along the way, there is so much we can and must learn from each other. Thus, I honor and each and every one of you.

Along with my teacher, Shamar Rinpoche, it gives me great joy to dedicate The Ecology of Oneness to you.

Table of Contents

Preface

This book has been cooking in me for almost twenty-five years. Perhaps all my other books have just been a preparation to write this one. In 2006, being more incensed than usual regarding the political shenanigans in the world and the various disasters which were seemingly getting worse as a result of hubris and greed, my book, *The Buddha at War*, was my way of offering the wisdom I had been gifted by so many illustrious teachers in language that could help people grapple with the sadness, despair, and anger many feel when wanting to see positive, informed, and compassionate changes in the societies and nations they live in. From the enthusiastic response that book received, I was asked by the publisher if I could interview renown Buddhist Masters about their take on the issues of the day; poverty, corporate greed, arms proliferation, warfare, etc.. One may think that "holy" people would have little interest in the world of ordinary mortals. But, in truth, this is really their business and they need to be well informed. Thus was born *The Wisdom of The Buddhist Masters: Common and Uncommon Sense*. Inspired by these interviews and on the heels of the success of *The Buddha at War*, I wanted to lend my own voice to the throng and expand my vision in a new edition. Despite the fact that my teacher, Kunzig Shamar Rinpoche, liked my title and I would have preferred to keep it, the publisher wanted a less provocative title, which lead to the release of *The Buddha at War's* second edition as *Becoming Buddha*.

But, there was much more I felt I needed to share; some from my Buddhist training, but also from my life experience and exposure to many traditions and life experiences. Shamar Rinpoche must have known that this was an itch I needed to scratch. And in him casting me back out into the world, out of the security of the Buddhist enclave, I received the prompt and blessing to create *The Ecology of Oneness.*

I wrote this book on the fly. I knew what I wanted to say, made broad outlines, sometimes managed to write some post-it note sentences and a few paragraphs here and there. But unlike other times where I had more dedicated opportunity to write, the business of the world has all but consumed my time and I found that a rare quiet morning or sleepless night gave me the moments and space to finally get it all together.

Then, in the holding of this Oneness vision and reality, I have spent much of my writing time in social media, promotional campaigns, blogs and podcasts sharing thoughts on various subjects. Subsequent to this book, there is *Living in The Ecology of Oneness: A Guide to Survive and Thrive in Uncertain Times. Living in...* covers five years devoted to looking at ecological, political, psychological, general health, and spiritual issues. In most recent days, our global pandemic and the acceleration of ecological disaster – the two of which I see as being interdependent - stand out as a features driving the narrative and the vision as to where we go next along our way.

You will also note that the beginning of this book is autobiographical. But I do not look at this as being a memoir, but rather, a necessity to lay out the background from which I am writing. I am an American hybrid. And, in these times, and possibly forever, we are all hybrids of race, culture in the ever-moving reality of humans seeking home, solace, and purpose. Thus, my own journey is an allegory of the times we are in, hence a useful example to reflect upon and use as a re-assurance to you as you learn to live more fully your own truth.

I mention many friends and teachers in this book. My thanks come in sharing their wisdom – which is something every teacher hopes will happen with what they convey to others.

But, more importantly, I am indebted to my muse, my Beloved Melanie, who has faced recent tragedies in her family life with a grace, grit, and open heart that has proven her to be a warrior priestess and a partner I feel honored to stand beside. Although she has not written a word in this book, in the hum and silence of our togetherness, I know we stand united in this vision of *The Ecology of Oneness*.

Robert Sachs

Introduction

Oneness, Heresies, and a Possible Future

The pop culture of the post-millenial world has created a two-word mantra, repeated by spiritual teachers, actors, eco-activists, rock icons, and new age pundits; that mantra is ...

WAKE UP!

Waking up, awakening, seeing the light, enlightenment... These words and phrases have been used by spiritual leaders and the teachings of the world's great religious and wisdom traditions for centuries. It is a call to awaken from slumber; a slumber of unconscious living and the sleepwalking that many if not all of us end up doing to a greater or lesser degree as we move through our days. This lack of consciousness in our daily lives has biological, emotional, relational, social, political, and ecological consequences. Not being fully conscious of who we are and what we are a part of in the vastness of the fathomless sky, we get fixated on only a small portion of that vastness, attaching our lives, our meaning, and ultimately our happiness to a fraction of the picture both within us and around us. And then, in the onslaught of change that inevitably cascades into our lives from moment to moment despite our efforts to hold on to what we've grasped, we get angry, disappointed, defensive. In the mind science as taught by the Buddha, there are Three Poisons we contend with: ignorance, attachment, and aggression. We don't know what is going on. We think we know what is going on. And, we get annoyed or angry with anyone who disagrees with us. This happens in our personal lives, our societies, even between nations. At the root of our suffering, our pains, our conflicts, there are these three, these Three Poisons that act like a, numbing narcotic that dulls our mind, our senses, and emotions.

To "wake up!" then is to wake up from the intoxicating stupor of these poisons. Through being taught practices of contemplation, prayer, and meditation, the spiritual traditions of the world have endeavored to widen our horizons, free us of holding on so tight, and find peace within and without. Such methods appear to be the universal approaches most effective for human consciousness to progress and grow. And over the course of history, the traditions teaching and refining these methods have emerged all over the world on every continent in almost every possible terrain: jungles, river banks, mountain caves, deserts, plains, and islands.

These traditions have always served a dual function in society. For the many, men and women recognized as the spiritual or wise ones were sought out for guidance and answers to questions from the most basic day-to-day issues to existential dilemmas. They provided answers, codes of conduct, and values to keep peace and harmony amongst the collective. This proved useful, sometimes in general, other times for the benefit of one side or another. In either case, these traditions functioned to exert or legitimize forms of social constraint and control for the "common" good.

At the same time, there has always been a revolutionary dimension or potential to these traditions. This is because that as much as there is the need for there to be stability in society, those who are more awake can see the constant changing nature of life. Wars, weather, pestilence, famine, the march of our bodies from birth towards death speak to the truth of impermanence and the need to adapt, to see anew, and envision a possibly different future. Thus it is that priests, rabbis, shamans, sages, and elders of the world's cultures have revealed deeper and more profound wisdom to diligent ones seeking to join their ranks or replace them as the elders of their family, clan, or lineages. As novices, neophytes, apprentices, monks, nuns, and yogis-in-training, these individuals are encouraged to wake up; to see the world as it really is and their place in it. This does not mean to say, however, that each of these traditions teaches the same things or have come to the same conclusions. The general idea was to see the world from a larger perspective and know our place in it and how to access all of our potentials. Like any endeavor, the results of the contemplations, prayers, and meditations varied, depending on the capacity and intentions of those who practiced what was taught to them as well as by the capacities and intentions of the teachers. Thus, there would be some who would be well-indoctrinated, emerge from such training and take their place as the next shaman, the next, priest or rabbi. But, there have always been those who have penetrated even further into the mystery of it all and emerge from such training with new, revolutionary ways of seeing the world. Even on the road to waking up there have been party-liners and heretics. At this time, I contend that we are in the age of the heretic.

Heresy and Oneness

One of the hallmarks of heretics over the centuries is that they usually grow beyond or transcend whatever the tradition is that they started in. They begin to see a universality; a oneness of heart, spirit, and substance that links us biologically, emotionally, and spiritually with each and every being on this planet - and beyond. While the paths of the traditions may circumscribe their own goals in terms of who is and who is not considered and accepted as a true devotee or follower within the societal framework in which they function, there are those who take the methods taught that appear to be universal, working with the body, the mind, and the breath that binds them as one – and go further, embodying, rather than merely representing, the teachings they have received. Such individuals don't always start off with this intention or direction. But time, circumstance, and awareness come together yielding unexpected results.

In a time when the average person stayed, lived, and died within a five mile radius of where they were born, which was pretty much the case for most of humanity until the last 150 years, the traditions that provided stability and the possibility to awaken functioned amongst relatively stable, homogeneous populations. This world is virtually non-existent today. Thus, along with the rare breed of heretics that sometimes come along to shake up the spiritual and social fabric of their communities, the spiritual and social fabric of our times is already rocking and rolling quite noticeably. Despite the efforts of those who see as their mandate stability in such spheres, even the average person reels from "TMI" (too much information) producing in its wake questions and doubts that previous generations may not have been so acutely aware of. Though they may not say this of themselves, I see everyday people as heretics in their own right. They want to know what is going on. And those trying to maintain societies' infrastructures don't seem to be able to come up with solutions to the diversity of problems that ooze through the cracks of the structures we assume as more solid than they ever are. Despite even the efforts of the very wise, the priests, masters, gurus whose messages often attempt explain to people that the relative world around them is like a dream – ephemeral – and ever changing, the sheer weight of factors contributing to the slippery slope of our modern world, factors which will be elucidated in coming chapters, presents more questions than answers. In part, I contend that some of this has to do with a growing breed of human that can best be described by the not-so-attractive term of "mongrel."

Today, more and more of us humans on the planet are mongrels. Cultures, races, religions, sexes, classes and castes have fewer and fewer places where they exist in isolation, in tact, or homogeneous. A long history of personal and collective factors - in transportation, commerce, environmental displacement, wars, wanderlust, the influence and presence of technology and media, and the dream of new possibilities have together spawned a breed of humanity whose borders and boundaries at the physical, psychological, spiritual levels are more asynchronously bumping up and melding with one another more than in any other time in our history on this planet.

Cities have always been melting pots. America has been termed the melting-pot nation. My contention is that in this time, the pot is melting *everywhere* and it is melting faster and the ooze of fusion is melting tribes and clans that at one time were the embracing societal structures for families, world-views, cultural and religious beliefs. As a result, a new kind of tribe is emerging. It is in many ways a "tribeless" tribe; one that can only survive and be sustainable if our human tendencies for creating mental, spiritual, and cultural boundaries are not used as walls of exclusivity, self protection, and disproportionate appropriation of what others need. This new tribe is being called on to transcend boundaries, to explore what is commonly shared and good between us, while at the same time celebrating the many historical and cultural influences which have given the human family such a phenomenal array in which we display our creativity, our love of life, meaning, but most of all the deep-seeded longing for community, communal experience, and transcendence of the personal. This amorphous tribe of heretics and seekers are commonly rooted in an awareness of inter-connectedness and inter-dependence; in *oneness*.

This is the tribe of *oneness*, a tribe with a perspective that transcends tribalism. This *oneness* is not an amalgamation of this and that, a kind of soup, which a friend of mine calls "newage." The growing number of people with this *oneness* perspective wants to be mindful, engaged, and connected to what is authentic *and* relevant. In a world where so much of what we have often been taught to assume about life and the world we live in is no longer absolute, but relativized, this *oneness* tribe fosters critical thinking skills and the ability to become better individual meaning-makers. This does not mean that such people disavow their connection to whatever their religion, faith, or philosophy has been or currently is. Rather, with a premium on connection, these are people who do not feel threatened by those around or among them who hold to different ways, worldviews, or religions. They celebrate and may even participate in new and different ways as a part of the willingness to learn, embrace, and grow together. As such, they share local and global concerns with a human family that cherishes the land and the world that supports and nourishes us and the many ways we live on it and amongst each other to ensure the same for future generations. They value tradition and understand the power of ritual, but are not shackled by blind allegiances or a lock-step mentality. They want to maintain, perhaps return to, but certainly wish to promote values and morals that reshape our educational systems, commerce, and politics to support and uplift all sectors of society. The goal of this upliftment is intrinsically altruistic: to foster a more mature and truly equanimitous way of caring for the greatest possible number of beings we share this planet as the norm rather than an unrealistic ideal or exception.

Oneness vision is implicitly ecological, recognizing the absolutely essential and necessary relationship that must be wedded between how we think, feel, and act in relation to the natural world around us and all of its plant and animal life. It is a vision focused on the long-term sustainability of humanity and the planet we as humans inhabit. For the Ecology of Oneness and the Oneness tribe is not just about us humans learning how to get along. **At this point, we can no longer tolerate or** condone any doctrine or dogma that merely sees the natural world and its inhabitants as a supermarket of commodities to be taken at will, consumed, and trashed. Not having a perspective that understands that we are all in this together has reached a point that is not only illogical, but lethal.

In this book, I shall share with the reader my own story. In some ways it is unique. After all, it is my story. But, I contend that there are many of us who have lived in one tradition or another, have gone to parochial schools, been educated in whatever faith we were born into, or have gone through transformational experiences through whatever life has lain before us and have felt the need to know more. Our awareness, education, and sensitivity has made us conscious of something more, different, perhaps more meaningful, and at the same time difficult to explain or share with those who still see themselves more comfortably within the structures and cultures of today teetering so precariously. Thus, my story – our stories - epitomize why the tribe of Oneness is emerging, what forces, pro and con, contribute to this, and what steps and stages in thinking and intention we need to embrace for this growing number of tribeless tribesmen to be a relevant and sustainable force for good on the planet in the years to come. As a writer who has interviewed wise spiritual leaders for my previous works, I do not see what is emerging in the rank and file of such individuals or the loose collective they may be identified with as the dominant or majority force or human presence leading us into a resurrection of the heyday of materialism. We've been there, done that, and are done with that. And what is the heart and motivation of this tribe of Oneness certainly does not seek its inspiration from such. Like the elders I sat with, I see and contend that we are going through major planetary shifts in ecology and human interaction that will not allow us to successfully return to the mid-twentieth century materialistic promises. Those days are gone and any attempts to force things back in that direction will be pushed back on by both the forces of nature and the growing sensibility in our human family. As more and more infrastructures that have either been propped up by, or have been created to support, the disparity in what this planet affords each and every being crumbles, the wisdom and potential for action in this tribe of Oneness will become more and more relevant and called upon.

A Free World?

To get the fullest sense of the title of this book, I need to comment on the phrase "Free World."

In the twentieth century and no doubt even today, the "free world" means the West. Proponents of this conceptualization of how the world is divided have drawn an invisible line between what they define as the totalitarian governments of Eastern Europe and Eurasia and the democratic nations of the West. As corporations and plutocrats embed themselves in each and every government where product, profit, and power are what keep the wheels of our consumer based civilization spinning, I do not see "free" or freedom as part of the agenda. If anything there is a shrinking of the rights of individuals, a watching and marshaling of collectives that seems unstoppable. In this sense the historical notion of the free world in this context seems more like quaint vapid rhetoric.

Thus, what I mean by a "free world" is this.

We are more consciously aware as a species that there is no absolute view held by any tradition, be it religious, cultural, or societal that explains it all. We have created a world where virtually every dimension of our reality from the most basic to etheric levels is up for grabs and can be defined or justified in any number of ways. And, there are more people on this planet who are freer to do so than in any other time in history. Although we may not want this, it is so and thus we have no real or imagined security blanket to curl up in – at least for very long.

This is liberating and terrifying. For the individual to be able to choose what to believe and what one wants on so many levels in so many sectors of life can be overwhelming. I have called this the tyranny of freedom. While this may not be so for the many who exist below the poverty level or in lands of extreme suppression of personal freedoms, there are many who suffer anxiety, even mental paralysis in not knowing what or who to believe, how to take care of their body, what to eat, and so on.

And for those who want to maintain social control or exert power and/or influence, this wide-open field, where people are cut adrift and searching amongst the myriads of options before them, creates a two-edged sword. On the one hand, with the right marketing strategy, whether it be a carrot, a stick, or a slick combination of both, you can herd a larger sector of the populace for profit, for war, or other self-serving ambitions. But, if the calculations and prods are wrong for the

22

circumstance and time, where dissatisfaction outweighs the attempts to keep people placid and compliant, there could also be the largest civilian uprising that the world has ever seen.

The bottom line: We have more choices. How and what are we going to chose?

In the evolution of my thinking, contemplations and meditations that have brought me to this place in my own development, I have been touched by, broken bread with, been blessed by, and done ritual with those whose heritages I share genetically, have culturally lived amongst, or intentionally embraced. And there are many beautiful people along the way who have inspired me and fostered the confidence and certainty I have that the unified and holistic vision of Oneness is a worthy and a sustainable direction for those who feel so moved to recognize and identify their experience as what makes a part of the growing numbers.

I am a mutt, a product of the American religious and cultural experience. I know that I am not alone in this. For in these "interesting times," there are those of you who are Jews, Protestants, and Catholics whose journey has led you to India, Nepal, Tibet, and Japan to become Buddhists and Hindus. Some may claim to be "recovering Catholics" or escapees from the fundamentalisms of their families. Others of you claim to be atheists or agnostics, not because you reject all things spiritual, but because the religious contexts in which spirituality has been culturally defined for most of us has proven itself lacking, if not bankrupt. And, there are those of you still in your faiths of origins whom have dared to dive deeper than the parochialisms you were inculcated with when you were children and have emerged with greater clarity and an inclusivism that bespeaks the promise of Oneness. In fact, it is the awareness of the truth of Oneness where the hopes and dreams of a possible future of this disparate band, this tribeless tribe, converge.

In the story I am about to share, I identify with the various names I have been given along the way.

My parents named me Robert Michael Sachs. In a country that calls itself Christian, you could say this is my Christian name – even though my family is Jewish. Etymologically, it means "scholar, in the image of God, who has been martyred"- a weighty name with a story behind it. Professionally I am known as either Robert or Bob. Friends from Australia and New Zealand call me Rob. One aunt and people who don't know they are annoying me call me Bobby.

At my bris (circumcision), the attending Rabbi gave me the name Eliyahu Ben Tsvi, which I believe means Elijah Son of The Moose. Elijah is my favorite Hebrew prophet. I think it is grand that he is invited to every Jewish table at Passover. And Bullwinkle is one of my favorite cartoon characters.

Tibetan lamas have given me 3 different names; Karma Sonam Wangchuck (the activity of powerful merit), Norbu Wangyal (powerful wish-fulfilling jewel), and another name I am not suppose to utter while I remain in this body.

And in a Lakota naming ceremony, I have been made a member of the Bear clan, to whom I am known as Walking Thunder Bear. I seem to identify with this name more and more and enjoy the acronym "WTB."

On any given day, in any given moment, I see the value and power in each name I have been given. In the tribe of Oneness, I summon the power and blessing from each name I have been bestowed.

Chapter One

My Story

I am standing at the edge of a tide pool, overlooking the vast deep-blue expanse of the Pacific Ocean. In the course of preceding weeks, my wife, Melanie, and I have done a memorial for her sister, Elizabeth, who jumped to her death after years of mental pain and anguish. And we have just returned from a ceremony and celebration of the passing of a dear friend, who was slammed into by a truck as he overtook another on his bike ride to work through the redwoods he so loved. In the immensity of a deep sadness that makes the colors of my world seem muted, I feel raw and silent. No internal dialogue, my mind is silent – as if waiting.

In this moment, I see a seagull enter the periphery of my left eye, its wings moving just enough to keep its glide over the waves smooth and even. And as it moves from my left eye to my right, I feel the beat of its wings moving from left to right through my heart. And I lose a sense of what is inside and outside. My heart is the waves and the sky. The seagull and its flight joyfully whisper of intimacy where no separation exists.

A numinous moment. In the presence of the births of my children with Melanie and the many deaths I have witnessed as a hospice social worker, I have had other such moments that bespeak the same truth. But, in the sadness of this particular moment I was open and vulnerable, allowing the truth of Oneness to be etched upon my heart. And it is from this heart space that I share with you my story.

The story of me awakening to the truth that I am – in the words of the Christian Mystic Pierre Teilhard de Chardin – "a spiritual being having a human experience" is told here through various lenses of my life experience along with the religious and secular education I have taken along the way. What I encountered will lay a foundation for the history of my spiritual process as it has unfolded and led me to a personal awareness and commitment to an Ecology of Oneness.

Experience is colored by perception and perception is colored by education, be it formal or day-to-day cultural exposure, and events, again both personal and collective. It would be a sign of me either being intellectually immature or psychotic if what I believed about the world around me when I was fifteen would be the same when I am now over sixty. I think it thoroughly bizarre that people running for office have their opponents or media read back to them essays they wrote in their first year in college and are judged on this as being hypocritical or untrustworthy because time and maturity has led them to change their mind. This probably accounts for why we get the leaders that we do.

Along with the various significant others who came into my life as family and friends, there have also been numbers of religious and spiritual teachers from a number of western and eastern traditions who have inspired and influenced me either by their teachings and/or personage. I also hold a bachelor's degree in comparative religion and sociology and a Masters in Social Work. Thus studies like religious anthropology, the sociology of knowledge, social psychology, various models of psychotherapy, and history of religion all interface in my psyche along with everything else – hopefully in a way that you will find interesting, useful, and sometimes even, I hope, thoughtfully amusing.

This last point, "thoughtfully amusing," may seem odd when I wish to address our deepest spiritual yearnings and the quest each one of us is on – regardless of whether we know we are on it or not - but, I firmly believe that most of the time, no matter how strict or regimented we are in our quest, we are just muddling through. In our more materialist-based culture where various carrots of acquisition or achievement are dangled before us, even in our more spiritual yearnings about our place and purpose in life, we are encouraged to reach for a goal that some try to convince us is somewhere else; like some priceless spiritual bauble. At some level in our being, we know better. But in our uncertainty, we allow ourselves to get hoodwinked into this way of thinking. The problem with this approach is that over time, it seems to reinforce an exaggerated sense of self-importance; a "me" that is on a spiritual quest, which if we do and say all the right things, will identify us amongst others as a "spiritual" person. With myself and others who I have observed over time on whatever path they have been on, such an approach eventually leads us towards greater personal impoverishment. Consequently, when slowly – if ever – we wake up to our own holy shenanigans and find an authentic pathway of awakening, we suddenly become so much more aware of our own folly and foolishness. The divine drama lightens to become the divine comedy - and the person who has been fooling us the most has been us. Humility and humor, are indeed two of the most important ingredients, especially in the final furlongs towards awakening.

So, let me entertain you with my multi-faceted, multi-dimensional story with all the blemishes and foolishness in full view. And, while I do, I invite you to reflect on your own birth-to-this-moment journey. Also consider the connection to the land and places, and times, through which you have passed. For, very quickly we are losing an appreciation of the impact these have upon us – especially when our genetics and psycho-social-cultural influences come from the ancestors who were born, lived, and died hither and yonder.

As is the case for anyone who is not a Native American, my parents came from immigrant stock. My father was from a long line of rabbis. My great grandfather from my father's father's side, Zechariah Sachs, was a renowned rabbi in the Midwest. His son, Max, was as much a socialist as he was a Jew, so he became a dentist, while his brothers became bootleggers in the 1920's. You can thank them for the splendor and many social contributions of Las Vegas.

This lineage of rabbis was German for many generations, but lived in Romania as Jews were not allowed to own land in Germany. Jews were still expected to live amongst themselves, but often encountered other eastern European and Asiatic influences, with many encounters not being of a pleasant sort. Mongolian invaders and the pogroms (ethnic cleansing) in the mid- 1800's explain why my grandfather had very dark skin and almond-shaped oriental eyes. And many of the photos I have seen of my other ancestors from that same time period reveal squat, almost Native American looking relatives from his generation and before. In the progeny spawned from rapes came children whose genetic and cultural influences brought together Jewish, Christian, Shamanic, and Buddhist parentage.

My father's mother Helen – on the other hand – was more a blend of Lithuanian, German, and Semitic blood lines. They came from Germany directly to the US in the early 1900's, around the same time as my father's father. The two of them met in Cleveland which had a growing Jewish community. Married around 1915, my father, Sherman, was born in 1918. They lived on Cleveland's east side.

My mother's lineage had also been influenced by Euro-Asian races. My mother's mother, Rose, who equally looked somewhat Asian, had escaped the pogrom of Bialystok, Poland in 1906. During the pogrom, where over 80 were slaughtered and another 80 badly injured, my grandmother, presumably from one of the more influential families in the Jewish community, was hidden from the soldiers and mobs to keep her safe. Once the coast was clear, she escaped and eventually made her way with some of her relations to America. They, too, settled in Cleveland.

My mother's father had a more colorful background. Shmulke or Sam Bordo's great-grandfather had – in fact – originally come from Bordeaux, France. As an officer in Napoleon's army, after the French had lost to the Russians in 1812, many French soldiers, including my injured great-great-great grandfather, stayed in and around Russia. GGG Grandfather Bordeaux had been injured in Latvia and was nursed back to health by a Jewish widow whom he eventually married. He was Roman Catholic, but no one seemed to mind because in those days, being a widow meant that you were thenceforth, un-marriable. By the standards of the times, he was doing her family a service by getting her off their hands. Like the Jews of Poland, the Latvians had similarly experienced the raping and pillaging of the Cossacks in pogroms, thus oriental and European bloodlines were part and parcel of the eastern European and especially the Jewish experience.

Eventually one of sons of the French Bordeaux and his widow bride got married and as Judaism is passed through the maternal line, the family he raised was Jewish. The "eaux" of Bordeaux was shortened and made easier for the Lett, Yiddish, and German languages of the region – hence Bordo. That said, the French officer's widow bride had children of her own. Thus, some were exclusively Jewish by blood, other were mixed.

Along with a very mixed heritage, my grandfather's early life was tragic in many respects. Though raised in a poor peasant family that made every effort to get their son educated, by the time my grandfather was 12, it became a reality that he need to help support them all. He was trained as a tinsmith and soon joined with other workers and the local farmers of the area in the socialist movements of the region. At 14, he witnessed beatings and murders at the hands of Cossacks who hunted down socialist sympathizers. He also saw how those who betrayed the movement were similarly dealt with, and was privy to the assassination of locals whose bodies were buried in the woods. By the age of 15 he was on the run, escaping through St.

Petersburg to Finland, then on to Stockholm, Baltimore, and eventually to Cleveland. He soon took a job as a tinsmith and got involved with the socialist politics of the early 1920's. I learned only recently is that the reason he spoke English with an Irish brogue was because he went to work for two tinsmiths by the name of Donnelly. He met my grandmother, Rose, who was a friend of his sister. After a traditional courtship of the time, they married and began their long line of progeny – eight – with my mother, Thelma, being the fifth.

While my parents, Sherman and Thelma, were both raised on the east side of Cleveland, they did not meet there, but rather at Ohio State where both were students. Typical of their times, a marriage was arranged at the completion of my father's veterinary degree. My mother stopped her schooling at that time to become wife and soon a mother. This was towards the end of World War II. After a stint with UNRA (the United Nations Rehabilitation Association responsible for re-seeding the devastated livestock supply of Europe), my father and mother eventually settled in rural Ohio, just outside of Cleveland; close, but just far enough away to be out of their parents' influence as well as the cloistered culture of Cleveland's Jewish community. While socialism was a strong value in both of their families, both my parent's had and remained politically progressive. They saw themselves as more culturally than religiously Jewish. With this idealism they had tried to live further afield – in Wisconsin, but found that German Americans of the region shared similar anti-Semitic sentiments to their European brothers and sisters. Rural Cleveland did not pose such problems for them and their young family - just yet.

The little town of Brecksville, Ohio, is where I was conceived. Go back two hundred years and where I was conceived, born, and raised for the first 5 years of my life was precious land to the Native Americans of the Midwest. "Ohio" means "great river" in Iroquois and was home to the Hopewell, then Miami and Shawnee. My first home overlooked the Cuyahoga River Valley, known to be inhabited since 200BC. The road that passed before our house was Chippewa, another name for Ojibwe, the largest group of Native Americans north of Mexico.

Here I was, the product of a multi-racial, ethnic, and religious stock, born into one of the more precious lands of First Nation people. Before I ever knew that my seemingly oriental and Mongolian features were from similar indigenous people of Asia or that I was Jewish living in a predominantly Christian community, I was just a little boy connecting with the elements of nature on native soil. What I remember of this time is rather idyllic. A neighbor had tied a rope to a tree that swung out over the ravine that led down to the Cuyahoga. A rope's length suspended over the tops of the trees below me, I reveled in space. I climbed trees, mostly young, but very tall saplings and would let the wind whip me to and fro on their very bendable top branches.

And, then there was the cemetery, right next to our house and my father's animal hospital. Who knows how many native people had lived and died on this land. But now, as consecrated ground for burial since the mid 1800's for "civilized" folk, I looked forward to the days when the gravediggers would come by to prepare a plot for an upcoming funeral. I would beg them to throw me into the six-by-six hole. And, I would lie down, close my eyes, and smell the earth around me. (At this time, it probably comes as no surprise to the reader that I am a hospice social worker.)

The elements are sacred to First Nation people – as they are to the Asian cultures whose medical and spiritual systems I have studied and no doubt have connection to through my Mongolian ancestors and my O-positive blood. Some anthropologists have theorized of a link between the Mongolian peoples of Asia and Native Americans who came to the Americas via the Bering Strait. And my early relationship to this genetic strain and a closeness to the elements was completed with the many days I would spend at the local community swimming pool. In the water, I would submerge myself and stay in the watery silence until I absolutely had to come up for air. And when my skin became all wrinkled, I would lie out in the sun on the hot concrete and bake myself into the natural brown that bespoke my Mongol heritage. Later when traveling through Europe during the summers, I was frequently mistaken for being Native American.

These days of living and playing in the elements around me faded for many years as the acculturation and socialization processes of school played a larger part of my life. No longer the young and innocent savage, it was time for me to become "civilized."

34

Perhaps some children are more sensitive or intellectually aware at pre-school and kindergarten age. When it comes to my identity as labeled by the cultural milieu around me, I was not. I was just a kid going into kindergarten and first grade suddenly finding myself in a room with a lot more kids my age. In Brecksville, there were no African Americans, Asians, or Hispanics – just white people. Thus, race was not in my awareness radar in the least. And when it came to religion, it was all a blur. If there was any religious awareness at all, it certainly had little to do with dogma, doctrine, or prayer. Holiday celebrations were all melted together in my mind; Christmas with Santa Claus and a baby called Jesus, the Easter bunny, Halloween, and the dreaded Valentine's day when we were strangely obliged to send out heart candies and cards to each and every boy and girl as if to somehow render gender irrelevant at a time when all of us were just waking up to it.

And my Jewish heritage?

My mother's father had had the religious zeal of his youth dashed against the harsh realities of a collapsing Latvian economy, the rise of Communism, and the blood of his compatriots who dropped at his side in skirmishes with the czar's soldiers. As being a socialist or – for certain - a communist was not a label that was wise to carry during the forties and fifties, politically progressive with a smattering of Jewish custom probably best describes how my mother and her siblings were raised.

And, despite the noble lineage rabbis he was born into, my father was a bit jaded about Jewish orthodoxy. Whilst his father's brothers had gone into organized crime, my father's father was, again, more a socialist, but more insistent about keeping Jewish customs alive for his children. Although a dentist by profession, the rabbinic line of which he was a part came through in his fearless writings and actions in civil rights, economics, and political inequality in the land of the free. From such a background, I would say that my father was religiously ambivalent.

But, both he and my mother felt that despite their own reservations, it was important to provide their children with some religious heritage. Thus they embraced the growing Reform Jewish movement. What this meant for me was that I saw candles being lit on a Friday night, a prayer said in some foreign language that I did not understand, my parents drinking a bit of wine, and the occasional visit from aunts and uncles who had funny eastern European names and spoke a combination of English and Yiddish. When we got together with my cousins, what was more important was whether there was enough food and space to run around in.

Although I had older sisters, like most five-years olds, I did not pay much attention to what they did or what they were going through with their friends. For me, the first revelation that I was somehow different from the other kids around me came up when we moved into a new and prestigious housing development.

I do not know if I first heard the term "Jew boy" or the more offensive "kike" before or during my first fight where being Jewish somehow mattered. Not really knowing what being a Jew really meant and – reflecting on this time – I am not sure if even any of the boys who wanted a fight between me and my new neighbor knew what being a Jew meant either other than what their parents or some other significant person in their lives wanted them to believe. From around this time through the end of the fifth grade I became familiar with all the rumors; that Jews had horns, loved only money, ate young Christian boys and girls, and, the greatest of Jewish horrible deeds, killed Jesus. But here I was, literally pushed into a circle of excited, jeering boys wanting to see someone hurt; me, in particular. The neighbor boy had a birth defect that caused him to limp and have no use of one of his arms. I saw his disadvantage and did not really want to take a swing at him. But, he swung wildly at me, catching me in the pit of my stomach. Winded, I ran home and lay on the cool floor of our garage to let the aching subside. And then, I got up and went back to fight some more, this time to win. The boys didn't expect this and when it seemed that I might be able to hold my own and their local hero get a thrashing, they called the fight off. This was my welcome into the neighborhood.

And this is how it went for many fights during this time. There was even a time when it was clear that I was winning and the gang supporting their hero Jew-hater pinned me down to let him get the better of me.

Such incidents happened out of school, on the weekends, on summer break. In school, with classroom rules and teachers nearby, the antagonism was subtle. I lived under the tenuous illusion that I had friends. And the tenuousness of this was readily made apparent at Christmas and Easter time when, for a few weeks before and a few weeks after these holy days, many friends would not speak or play with me. After all, I had killed the Savior.

As the distinction of me as a Jew became a poignant awareness in my life, I began to wake up to humiliation and pain both of my sisters were going through. The older sister closest to me in age would be mocked, invited to parties that did not exist. My oldest sister – who was very beautiful – would be asked out on dates only to be dumped within a few dates when the boy's friends started calling him "rabbi."

My parents tried to be supportive through this increasing barrage of anti-Semitic sentiment. But, this all changed when my father's veterinary hospital was firebombed twice. We later learned that the arsons were significant citizens of our community. Police investigations led to no arrests, let alone convictions. A friend of our parents even knew who was involved, but would not step forward for fear that the same would happen to his business. Thus, my parents moved us to where they hoped we would all be safe – back into Cleveland's Jewish enclave. And we became more actively involved in the synagogue that my parents had joined while we were still out in Brecksville.

Although we had been members of The Temple on the east side of Cleveland for a couple years, being only ten, I never sat with my parents or sisters in the main sanctuary during Sunday services. Children my age were read Bible stories in the library. Perhaps it was engrossing enough for some of the kids. But I was a country boy. I liked air and space and earth and fire. Every chance I could I would go to the bathroom, escape out into the halls, run up and down the many staircases. And most often, I was eventually caught and hauled back into civilized captivity.

But, my feelings of agitation and distraction were interrupted in one moment of what I can now call an experience of transcendence.

I am not sure why the particular incident in which this moment occurred happened. Perhaps it was just one of the special events that the teachers of the Sunday school arranged. In any event, we were given the opportunity to go into the main sanctuary before the service.

Lined up, we walked in a single file through a row of pews. The room was warm, the domed ceiling lofty. The pews smelled of varnished wood and well sat-in fabric. Prayer books were neatly tucked into the shelves that were fastened to the back of each pew to ensure that whoever sat behind that pew had their own book. The books were solid black, the paper thin and musty. And the air was resplendently silent.

Whether we actually stopped in our line up or kept walking, for me time seemed to slow down as if to meet with space in the stillness. And in the gap between moments, I felt something. What it was I can not rightly say. It just was. And it was exquisite.

Was this a glimpse of the divine; of God? Even though the teachers I listened to every week would tell me about God and his glories, I could not rightly say that that exquisiteness was or was not God. For me it did not matter. It was just an honest, genuine moment. And, it has been the honesty and genuineness of that moment that has been my reference point for all religious and spiritual pursuits ever since.

It wasn't very long until I started to have other experiences like this – but not in temple. In a nearby Catholic church, the altar of marble and gold with the looming Christ on a cross kindled the same fire. Later in my teens, at the Sistine Chapel, again, the same. One could argue that this was all a part of the early pubescent experience. But, I have had similar experiences in my twenties, thirties, and forties, and fifties; at my first Tibetan Buddhist retreat center, at the chalice well in Glastonbury, at Corn Rock in Arizona's Second Mesa Hopi site, and nowadays, just looking at the ocean, a clear blue sky, or in the eyes of a baby.

When I had my first moment like this, did this mean that my wandering in the synagogue halls stopped? No. Did it mean that I became a model religious devotee? Hardly. In fact – if anything – it pushed me past or perhaps egged me on in what seems to be a nascent spiritual life rife with sacrilege - depending on your viewpoint.

From The Temple's standpoint, I was a holy terror. While I had felt an awe and presence in the personage of Rabbi Abba Hillel Silver, the chief rabbi of the synagogue and one the great Jewish luminaries of the twentieth century, his son, Rabbi Daniel did not particularly like my influence in the religious high school program. With a group of fellow renegades mutually sharing the motto, "Dismantle but do not destroy." We went out of our way to make learning Hebrew or Jewish history more entertaining. I think the impetus to be subversive stemmed from two sources. One was my observation of how little attention the attending adults gave to the religious service and sermon compared to their business dealings before and after the service. They were like moneylenders in the Temple of Jerusalem. Didn't they feel what I felt in the sanctuary?

But beyond this sense of moral outrage – if I really had any at all – was just my spoiled upper middle class sense of privilege playing itself out in any number of pranks; taping the chapel organ keys together, unscrewing light fixtures and wall plates in the stair wells, and probably most sacrilegious, putting a bottle of wine in the Ark of The Covenant – the holy of holies. And, as breakfast was always served before class, we would smuggle bags of bagels and brownies into class to pass around when our teacher turned to write on the board.

Finally, Rabbi Dan had had enough. Coming to our class, the hooligans were taken out into the hall and told that we were expelled. Had it not been for a sympathetic younger rabbi, Lawrence Forman, this would have been our fate. But, Rabbi Forman's gentleness and – perhaps – remembrance of his own rebellious younger days gave him the patience for our adolescent stirrings, knowing that this approach would keep us connected to what was spiritually good beneath our vandal-ous ways. Interestingly enough, that which is spiritual has remained the focus and thrust for the three of us who were the main conspirators of the time.

While my life in temple high school continued and was thus growing my Jewish identity, I was also used to feeling like a minority. I had been a minority of one. As such, it only stands to reason proven over the course of my life that I was socially conditioned to act like and identify with being and seeing eye-to-eye with others in the same predicament. This way of seeing the world and understanding the plight of others in social and cultural situations not that dissimilar to my own has remained a crucial part of my identity. Thus at home, around the neighborhood, and in school I would not say that I was so self-conscious in my adolescence that I went out of my way to find friends who were Catholics, Protestants, or African Americans. But find them I did. And to my dismay, rather than me receiving the brunt of kids calling me Jew Boy or kike, I heard Jewish kids around me refer to my friends in derogatory Yiddish terms. "Goyim" is a term which denotes someone not learned in the Torah or Talmud, the sacred texts of Judaism. It is a term of condescension. An unlearned Jew could be a Goy, but I never heard this term used in any other way than to derogatorily refer to a Gentile. Boy goyim were "shagitzes." Girl goyim were "shiksas." African Americans, then called Blacks or Negroes, were "shvartzas." My friends were not subjected to the physical attacks I endured and I am not even sure whether they knew what was being said or the derision that came from such terms. But, it cut through me like a searing knife. It made me embarrassed and at times ashamed to be a Jew. But beyond that, it taught me a lesson that is the backbone of my identity. And, it became clarified to me years later in the story of the historical Buddha.

The historical Buddha was originally Siddhartha Gautama, the princely son of a powerful king. In his day, wars fought in the name of religion, just like in the

Crusades. One king or tribe would subscribe to the dogma of this or that priest's interpretation and explanations of the attributes of God (Brahma), what they liked, who was in, who was out. Infidels, those not of a similar faith needed to vanquished in any number of ways, from pleasant discourse to – if need be – annihilation. When he saw this, Siddhartha came to a very sane, pragmatic realization. If God is an objective truth, why are there so many interpretations on who or what he or she is? Furthermore, what sense is there in killing each other based on these subjective interpretations? The conclusion he came to was: Let's not concern ourselves with God. Rather, let us examine how we come to our opinions. Let us examine our own mind and emotions. He did not deny the reality of God, but saw it as irrelevant until we came to know ourselves. Thus Buddhism is not atheistic or in denial of God, but rather, non-theistic; a mind science more than a religion.

Not knowing this story when I was eleven years of age, my limited interpretation at the time was that no one or any one group corners the market when it comes to prejudice. There was prejudice in the Christian community towards Jews and there was prejudice in the Jewish community towards Christians and African Americans. The conclusion I came to was that if we were all ever going to get along, what we needed to do was understand and uproot prejudice.

The awe that I first experienced in the temple sanctuary may have been a guiding light in the back of my mind. But, in a way, it is inexorably fused with my identification and empathy for minorities and the disadvantaged of all persuasions. I was in the early stages of forging a heretical path that has inevitably and always offended sectarian biases and its proponents over the course of my life. It is my own path through the American experience and a core ingredient of the Ecology of Oneness.

As both religious and regular high school drew to a close, I entered Case Western Reserve University. My teen fascination with such revolutionary and minority writers such as Alexander Solzhenitsyn, William Stryron, Eldridge Cleaver, Richard Wright, James Baldwin, and the radical psychoanalytic writings of R.D. Laing lead me to chose a combined major of sociology and religion. The deeper I went into the study of religious history and experience, the more I wanted to pursue what a Jewish boy would pursue if he were to chose a religious life. My plan was to follow in the footsteps of my ancestors. I would complete undergraduate work in the traditional four years and then apply to a Jewish theological seminary to become a rabbi.

Mind you, this is what I thought I had to do because in Cleveland, that's what spiritually oriented Jewish boys did. Yet, as a religion major, I was more interested in the existential literature of Camus and Sartre and mystical and transpersonal writings of Hindu avatar, Sri Aurobindo, the Theravadin Buddhist teachings in the Dhammapada, and the gnostic writings of early Christianity.

I loved studying such writings. But, in those days, there was also so much else happening on campus. Case Western was one of the hot spots for civil rights action and political protest against the war in Viet Nam. There were also lots of girls. And then, there was pot.

Over the years I have met so many parents who are squeamish about or outright lie to their kids about the fact that they inhaled. I did and have never hidden this fact from my own children. Did I smoke pot because of peer pressure? Well, my friends were doing it. But, they also drank and I didn't really like drinking at all. Was I depressed or emotionally bent out of shape? No doubt I was confused. I was eighteen and studying religion, psychology, sociology, and surrounded by radical hippies and new ways of thinking. And I was really beginning to enjoy and having a lot more sex. So, why pot? Perhaps I am just being superficial – not wanting to get down to the deeper meaning of it all. But to be honest, the main reason for pot was curiosity.

No one was holding a joint in front of me calling me a wuss or sissy or square. One evening in my dorm, sitting with a group of friends, I just reached over and took some tokes. And I watched my mind move in directions that were unfamiliar, yet pleasant. It was interesting. It was amusing. And for me, that was the point. I was not interested in the "scene" and social aspects of what may be called pot culture. And to be frank, I think there were many like me who experimented this way. And once they had the experience, it did not have to become a way of life. For myself, although I would continue to indulge in hash and marijuana for another two years, it was never a "gateway" to other drugs. And, in fact, my interest in it began to diminish after an incident that revealed to me another dimension of reality and the presence of those who inhabit such realities. Although this incident happened later on when I was studying in Europe, the case to make is worth stating here.

Having played music with a group of fellow musicians late into the night in a friend's dorm room, all of us were wasted on hashish and weed. At certain point, I felt compelled to lie down on one of the beds and retreat within myself from all of the sound, smoke, and conversation. The sense of contact with the mattress vanished and I was very aware of my body from head to toe.

Lying thus, I felt and then saw several ethereal ladies hovering over me, looking. And then one came close, brought her face close to mine, and breathed. It was a moment of exquisite joy – from which I soon awoke.

And to this day, after years of not indulging in any drug whatsoever since that time, these angels, dakinis, or whoever they are remain in the periphery of my mind. And, I honor them.

The writings of Aldous Huxley, Carlos Castaneda, and the early writings of Dr. Andrew Weil illustrated how cultures throughout history used mind-altering substances to elicit changes of consciousness. This was usually done in the presence of elders. And each culture that uses substances such as datura, marijuana, peyote for such purposes has admonitions for when these "sacred" substances are used irreverently or for recreation. Few read beyond the first two books of Carlos Castaneda who takes datura to perform miraculous feats and gain super-sensory awareness under the guidance of the brujo, Don Juan. But in book three, *Journey to Ixtlan*, Don Juan makes Castaneda do all these feats without the use of drugs. When asked why he no longer was using datura as part of the ritual, Don Juan tells Carlos that he no longer needs them. Casteneda presses the point – asking why he was encouraged to take them in the first place. Don Juan's reply roughly goes like..."Because you were such a block-headed idiot, I had to change the way you saw the world." Again Castaneda pushes further. What would have happened had he continued to take the drug? "That's simple," says Don Juan. "It would have killed you."

Tibetan lamas call marijuana medicine. It is for the mind that cannot free itself from fixation on views that limit reality. (At the time I had my numinous encounter with female deities, I only briefly knew of Tibetan lamas, but had not heard anything like this.) Ironically, if taken all the time, like the warnings of Don Juan, lamas say that our minds and the world we see begins to shrink in awareness and sensitivity. Later on, when I was doing my placement at a drug rehab center for my Masters in Social Work degree, the director of the facility, Ted, a very wise and insightful counselor, made comments to that effect. But he also went further. "Anything a drug can do, you can do better," he would tell his alcoholics and drug addicts. And, he would add, we are attracted and run the risk of becoming addicted to substances that reinforce the way our mind is already inclined. Depressives go for depressants, like alcohol and downers. Hyper individuals go for drugs that make them more hyper, like uppers and speed, and so on. In my own case, the pot seemed to accentuate a part of my level of perception that has always allowed me to step back and see a bigger picture. Over the next few years, what I learned that would become a part of my own spiritual practice made smoking pot irrelevant.

So, my pot smoking days were few. It did not take me long to know that the scene around drugs was not where I wanted my life to go. And soon after that experience, I was hitch hiking through Europe during Case's winter break.

As a young American traveling in the early seventies in Europe, drugs were everywhere young people were. But, perhaps my circumstances were a bit extreme. I hope you don't mind a nostalgic interlude. Mind you, there is a point to me telling you what follows.

Landing in Luxemburg with a friend from college, we were almost immediately picked up on the outskirts of the airport by an American GI in a Volkswagon van. He was headed to London. Not really having an itinerary on than just being in Europe, we thought London was a great idea. So we stayed with him; from Calais to Dover to London, arriving in Belsize Park. We then learned that the GI had been a mule bringing in a large stash of hashish from Afghanistan. And, he was delivering it to the Number One drug dealer in London at the time. An ex-foreign legion soldier, now known as the Spider, could provide you with pot, hashish, uppers and downers, and acid – all from the convenience of his flat.

The traffic in and out of the flat was constant. Exhausted from the travel, not knowing London at all, and being a bit curious to witness the epicenter of a drug scene that was far more colorful than my dorm back in Cleveland, my friend and I decided to pitch our sleeping bags on the flat floor. But, after two days of light intermittent sleep punctuated by people playing music at all hours of the day and night, doing uppers, then downers, then uppers again, helping out the occasional person freaking out on acid, we beat a retreat to one of my uncle's friends in another part of London. They were just alcoholics. After a few days of too much gin and wine we were off to Amsterdam. The student hostel was in the Red Light district. Between endless beckonings from exotic ladies posing in windows in most revealing ways and the incessant invitations to buy, buy, buy drugs, I was growing weary of the spectacle.

It was in this frame of mind that my friend and I stuck out thumbs out on one of the main roads leading out of Amsterdam. And as if it was déjà vu all over again, another Volkswagon van stopped. Driving it was a tall, slender man with long red hair and a beard – what a Clevelander like me had been culturally taught to think of as a hippie and more specifically, a Jesus freak. The door of the van opened and we didn't hesitate. We hopped in. My friend was exhausted and went into the back to rest as he had done some inhaling at the Amsterdam's Cosmos. I sat up front with the calm and very peaceful hippie.

He made no effort at conversation. Yet the silence was not pressured – like the awkward silence one often feels in some social circumstances. I didn't know his name, nor did I ever ask it. Neither did he of me. But, I still ventured to start up a conversation. Upon reflection, what is strange is that I am sure we talked all the way from Amsterdam to Paris. Yet I can recall only one or two minutes of our exchange. For these few minutes changed everything.

"Where do you live?" I asked.

"In a Tibetan Buddhist retreat center in Scotland" he replied.

"What's that like?" I enquired.

And, he said, "It's the kind of place where every time you turn a corner you walk into yourself."

And, in the moments that followed that one statement, I decided that I needed to go there.

When I got back to Case Western, I looked into a junior year abroad in the UK. I think I would have grabbed at any program in the British Isles. But, there just so happened to be a program with the University of Lancaster in England's Lake District; about sixty miles from the Scottish border and eighty miles from Kagyu Samye Ling Tibetan Buddhist Centre.

Although I had already set my intention to go to Samye Ling the first chance I had, once I was settled in and could get away from the University of Lancaster, another pivotal moment in the religious direction of my spiritual quest came just a few weeks before I left for the UK.

It was late September of 1972; the time of the Jewish high holy days, Rosh Hashanah (Jewish New Years) and Yom Kippur (The Day of Atonement). In my mind, I was still intent on going to rabbinical seminary after completing my undergraduate degree. My family knew this. But, more to the point, my girlfriend's family knew this and was excited to think of their future son-in-law as a rabbi.

My girlfriend was (and still is to this day) an extraordinary singer. As she had solos with her synagogue's choir for Rosh Hashanah, I was more than happy to accompany her, sit with my fellow Jews, and listen to her angelic voice.

Indeed, that evening her voice was angelic. Beyond her voice, though, I heard another call.

Listening intently to the prayers and sermon, gazing around me at the young and old, I somehow felt I was in the wrong place. This is not where I should be. This was not who I was. Or – should I say – neither the words, the people, nor my girlfriend's angelic voice could fully express or contain the full range of my feelings about myself and my relationship with whatever ineffable transcendental force I felt akin to.

It was at this point – in a synagogue during the middle of prayer at one of the holiest days of the Jewish calendar - that I decided I would never become a rabbi.

Did I feel a calling? Yes, but not to this. I did not have words to explain this to anyone at the time. So, I said nothing. But, I was relieved. At the end of the service I left the synagogue never to return as a practicing Jew.

This didn't mean that when I arrived in England that I went immediately to the Buddhist center I had been told about and become a Buddhist. I was just twenty in my first semester abroad. There was enough to do; pubs, hash, beautiful English women. Even my classes were interesting – when I woke up to go to them.

But, winter break came soon enough. Ten weeks after arriving in the UK, I was standing on the M6 motorway, hitching north. To get to Samye Ling took about 4 hours; sixty miles through the Lake District beyond Carlisle, then off onto winding Scottish roads to the wettest town in the British Isles – Eskdalemuir.

My last day at university before hitching to Samye Ling had been rich with every possible debauched delight. Like going from pitch darkness to total bright light, it was such a contrast to the quiet, contemplative, somewhat monastic aura of Samye Ling. Yet, it was exhilarating and I wanted to dive in and experience everything it had to offer. Having arrived in the mid-afternoon, I joined in on my first yoga class, then ate my first all vegetarian meal, then sat in my first Tibetan Buddhist puja (chanting meditation).

And then I went to bed for the next five days. A radical shift in perception and experience lead to a full-bodied systems failure. More than likely, it was the combination of the contrast between my college dorm life and the natural purity of simple retreat center living, the intensity of my spiritual yearning, and the power of the mantras, bells, and drums all culminating in a 104 degree fever and the need to sleep for several days. All I could do – all I wanted to do – when I was awake was have a bit of soup and sit in the meditation hall and listen to chanting. The morning chants to the goddess Tara, the afternoon chants and drumming to the wrathful protector Black Coat, the evening chanting to the compassionate Chenrezig – Loving Eyes – the chants felt like rain descending upon me, bathing me, leading me into a place that seemed so familiar. I felt like I was home.

Was it the total other-worldliness of this experience that mesmerized me? Was I a part of some guru conspiracy, of peer pressure by fanatics exerted over neophytes? Had I entered into a den of malcontents, hippies, and other disgruntled counter-culture kids? In the years that followed, this is what my parents wanted to believe of my interest of all things Eastern. They even had an ex-Moonie deprogrammer come to my wedding reception three years later to check me out and see if I needed to be benevolently kidnapped and brought back to the fold. Fortunately, he was arrested on kidnapping charges before such a plot could unfold.

More to the point for me then and even to this day, was that the ineffable quality I experienced in the temple sanctuary and in my early youthful immersion in the natural elements seemed to come together in a way of being exemplified in what I saw and experienced at Samye Ling; a lifestyle that focused on a natural diet, yoga, and forms of prayer. I did not see any of these things as being a statement against the culture in which I was raised, or against anything else for that matter. Rather, what Samye Ling showed me was how I could build a life that was more focused, more purposeful, more connected; organically coming to an experience of Oneness.

That these aspects came together at a Tibetan Buddhist retreat center and expressed through Buddhist spiritual practice may seem such a radical departure – especially if one were to assume me to be exclusively an American Jew who had just given up the idea of becoming a rabbi.

But – in truth – I am a mongrel and maybe this was my first true embrace of my American, melting pot roots. Besides, I did have Mongolian blood in me. There are traces of Asian Buddhism in my genetic being. Though culturally and societally defined as being a Jew, the many bloods of many lands runs through me. I never really abandoned my roots. I just chose a recessive strain.

Thus in 1975, after graduating from the University of Lancaster living and working in London for a year, on a return visit to Samye Ling, I decided to make a formal step into the Tibetan Buddhist tradition by "taking refuge" in the three Jewels; the Buddha, the Dharma (the Buddha's teachings), and the Sangha (the Buddhist community).

What this has meant to me over the years has evolved. Life experiences and the practice of mindfulness and compassion as the core of what it means to be a Buddhist have broadened my perspective and softened the parochial edges that often times are an attribute of neophytes.

In the process of discovering something of profound meaning in one's life, this parochial adherence to every particular is a hallmark that most succumb to in their process of exploration and discovery. This is especially true if there is any dissatisfaction with the culture one lives in and/or the degree to which one's own spiritual tradition has either appealed or disappointed. Thus the teachings, lessons, doctrine, or dogma one adopts are often almost impossible to separate out from the cultural attributes or life examples of those who inspire, teach, or initiate one into that new tradition. A very savvy Tibetan Buddhist master, Chogyam Trungpa Rinpoche, once said that he was amused by those who went to Japan to study Zen and returned thinking that to practice Zen, it was important to sit on a black cushion. Similarly, if the path one choses is centered around the life and example of a guru, neophytes will have the tendency to adopt the attitudes and demeanor of the guru as if doing so makes them fit better into the guru's world. And if the guru or teacher represents a tradition in need of followers, then much energy is expended to ensure that this belief or view becomes the ground for membership and all that that entitles one to. And it is usually the ardently devoted who are the enforcers of this unspoken mandate.

In my own case, in the beginning, all of these factors were at play. For certain, the other-culture-ness of the ritual, mannerisms, and appearance of the Tibetan form of Buddhism and the ease and mental focus and mastery of the Tibetan lamas I met held a strong attraction that affected my daily lifestyle and habits. Not that I dressed like a monk. Indeed, this was never to be my path. I married Melanie soon after becoming a card-carrying Buddhist (At the time, she was not.) and went on to have five children together. But I had protection strings around my neck and wrists, wore a mala, preferred a more Eastern appearance in my dress. I would do formal pujas (meditations and prayers) when I got up and in the evenings. I still do many of these things to this day. Probably it is my Mongolian karma. But I'm more relaxed with it all. While I don't dress so that way anymore, our house is a blend of modern Californian and English Victorian with a predominance of Tibetan religious paintings and decorations throughout. Such icons represent positive attributes to aspire to. I like that.

With respect to my own Buddhist path, again my understanding of the principles and practices have both molded and been molded by life's many experiences. For years I did define the Three Jewels, the Buddha, Dharma, and Sangha, in very parochial terms. The word Buddha means "Awakened One," someone who is enlightened. Although I enjoy Tibetan and Eastern iconographic description and depictions of what such a being looks like, I have seen or been with enough teachers who demonstrate such qualities to not expect them to appear in only one specific guise. Each of us has awakening potential and it is almost impossible for anyone who is not awake themselves to have the discernment to recognize who is and is not awake around them. Thus while there are some who wear robes who may well deserve the term "awakened," the Buddhas in our midst can be wearing a three-piece suit or overalls. In truth, people and opportunities that awaken us are around constantly.

Parochially, Dharma has been translated as "the Truth" when in fact a better translation is one that my good friend, Lama Ole Nydahl, prefers: "the way things are." The Dharma is about understanding reality and being able to discern what is absolute with respect to principles and relative with respect to application. Thus whereas a good Buddhist teacher may explain how the mind works and the mechanism of how phenomenon display themselves through the process of birth, maturation, and dissolution (or in the case of us humans, birth, sickness, old age, and death), this does not mean that a Tibetan monk will know how to help you in dealing with your children, taxes, your business affairs. The Dharma explains the mechanism of how things work. It is up to you to figure out how they apply to your life. In this respect, it may be of interest to note that in countries where there is Buddhism, there is no term for being a Buddhist. As Buddhism is non-theistic and more a mind science than religion based on principles or laws expounded in the Dharma, those who live by those principles are said to be living inside "the law." Those who do not are said to live outside of the law.

Then there is "sangha" or community.

In the beginning of my Buddhist journey, I thought of sangha only in terms of those who also identified themselves as Buddhists. And like any other human looking for connection and a sense of belonging, I wanted and tended to believe that the foibles and foolishness of group and community life and activity were not a part of the official Buddhist organizations, centers, and its members; that the mindfulness practices and focus on "benefitting all sentient beings" translated into association free from in-crowds, in-fighting, and political intrigue. Indeed, I know many people who look at the Buddhist community with rose colored sunglasses, think of H.H. Dalai Lama and then conjure in their mind some utopian Buddhist world where all such human confusion is transcended. We are all looking for heaven on earth. While many of the great teachers such as His Holiness are more or less above reproach, sadly, I must report that like any other group - religious, social, or otherwise - political strife, intrigue, sexual impropriety, financial dirty deals, and other forms of villainy are just as much a part of the Buddhist community as any other community. And even between sects, schools, and teachers parochial exclusivity persists. Thus I have found myself oft times questioning, even challenging the various powers that be, even in high places, and have had my share of heartbreak when I have been in the midst of or witnessed shenanigans veiling itself in the cloak of religious impeccability.

These days, while I find the form of prayers and meditations I do daily and my preferences leading me to be affiliated with a particular Tibetan Buddhist school, this for me is sangha with a small "s." Beyond this, the larger, big "s" sangha that I find and enjoy is people who have what for lack of a better term I can describe as heart and are trying to connect with people in a mindful, conscientious, and compassionate way; i.e. have a Oneness perspective. Thus I find myself outside of the "fold" in many circumstances and find greater contentment and joy relating to an ever-expanding group of eclectic spiritual aspirants who bring to dinners, gatherings, and prayer circles a number of prayers and practices that enrich the experience of our times together.

Although cited as one of the world's "great religions" by many theologians, by its own definitions, Buddhism is better classed as a mind science as mentioned earlier. Having had the great pleasure of discussing and hearing from the lips of great Tibetan masters thus, in claiming myself to be a "primarily" Buddhist means that although I am on fire with the principles and practices of deepening my own spirituality and helping others do the same, I can also say that I do not identify myself with any particular religion. This does not mean that I have rejected my Jewish roots. Rather, along with my Jewish roots, the enquiring methods of

Buddhism have opened me up to stay open to the various teachings and heartfelt expressions of religiosity and faith as I have encountered it over the course of my life. This has led to some rather wonderful encounters and experiences over the years. Along with being in the presence of, studying with and serving the highest of the high teachers of Buddhism, including H.H. 16th Gyalwa Karmapa, H.H. Dalai Lama, H.H. Sakya Trinzin, H.H. Dudjom Rinpoche, and Lopon Tenzin Namdak Rinpoche to name just a few, I have met great Native American elders such as Leon Shenandoah, Oren Lyons, Rolling Thunder, Bear Heart, and Winona LaDuke. I have had feathers waived over me by Baba Muktananda, been hugged by avatar Ammaji, witnessed the musings and kindness of Pir Vilayat, been serenaded to by Sri Chimnoy, and taught how to die consciously by beloved Dharma brother, Lama Ole Nydahl. I have witnessed or been in the midst of miracles and miraculous events where my three-dimensional linear rational reality was challenged to explain acts of nature, displays of powers by individuals, even the appearance of angels and other-worldly creatures while only under the influence of my everyday mind. I have met inspired Christians of almost every possible sect. I have even sat vespers with the monks of Thomas Merton's monastery in Trappist, Kentucky. With Jews, Hindus, Muslims and Sufis, Druids, along with those who profess being Wiccan, I have participated in countless ecumenical meetings, prayer circles, and ceremonies. In this melting pot of human goodness and experience, I have grown less cocky about my own path and have been inspired to even adopt practices that I have found useful for one reason or another. Seeing similarities more than the differences I feel joyful listening to a gospel choir, hearing sermons of such charismatics as Joel

Osteen and Michael Beckwith, receiving blessings from Hindu saints, dancing with pagans, sweating with Native elders, singing Hindu and Buddhist mantras with beloved friends and Osho devotees, Deva Premal and Miten, and standing at our front door with Jehovah's Witnesses talking about matters of faith and the fate of humanity. And as if to celebrate the rich diversity in my experience, I have become a Universal Life Minister – like John Wayne, Johnny Carson, and Bob Hope - and embrace Freemasonry as a vehicle for practical ethical and moral action and philanthropy in daily life and my service to the community of which I am a part.

For me to be touched by and connected to all these faiths and paths does not seem in my mind to be contradictory, personally confusing, or hypocritical. And, all of it has helped me to be with, minister to, pray over, even bless people in any number of circumstances; in my counseling to the distraught, leading meditations, conducting weddings or coaching someone to and through their final breath. It has led some to see me as a Buddhist teacher, whilst others have seen me as a priest or rabbi - all valid in my estimation given my mongrel heritage and genetics. Some friends affectionately refer to me as a Buddhist rabbi, but I personally prefer to identify myself as a transpersonal midwife.

In these times I see many friends struggling to find their identity in one tradition or another, thinking that their inability to do so or dissatisfaction to feel at home in their own or somebody else's tradition is an indication of a lack of character or an unsolvable spiritual malaise.

What I contend here is that the days of one tribe in one state with one church and one indisputable and unchallenged faith is long gone – if it ever really existed. More than in any other time of history there is a preponderance of people experiencing the truth of the fleeting nature of their very existence, both on a personal and collective level. We may have been asleep in the belief of a permanent me-ness in a permanent society on a rock solid biosphere. But, this has never been true. Many great thinkers, from scientists to philosophers to spiritual teachers tell that whereas we have always been in a state of flux from micro to macro levels of our life and in an ever expanding, transforming universe and all its possibilities, these times have made us more poignantly collectively aware of these facts than any other time in history.

As such, the challenge we are facing may be eliciting in some, but definitely challenge all to take an evolutionary leap. Today's religions, which have created or been a part of the division and alienation within and between cultures, societies, and nations need to modernize. The exoteric dimension, the rules and regulations of membership and salvation (which we shall discuss later) that have become problematic and unsuited to the melting pot world, needs to be de-emphasized and/or reconstructed with the help of the esoteric – more meditative, contemplative, and intuitive - wisdom each of these traditions often conceals. If the mainstream of these faiths can recognize and align itself with the emergent growth of interest in and respect for the universality of the esoteric, wisdom traditions, and the new discoveries in neuro-science, a new level of inclusivity and participation in meaning making for a dynamic sustainable future built upon an ecology of Oneness perspective is possible for a far greater number of people than if the division of old ways of thinking persists.

We are beings of ineffable suchness. The light we manifest reveals our presence. Our voice and the words we use are the purest expression of the impact we make in the world around us. This is who we are and have always been and it has been the illusion of separation, the focus of every wisdom tradition to dissolve, that has really been the only thing standing in our way to awakening. "Enlightenment" is waking up to this truth.

Lofty truths, perhaps. But, from the experiences, teachings, and numinous moments of my life to date, this is what I have come to know, trust, and act from. This is the foundation of the Oneness perspective I share here. And, I am certain that there are many reading these pages who can trace and identify in their own lives similar insights, pursuits, encounters set against the background of the Free World that beckons us to bring together and include the various aspects of our mongrel-like being and a world of others who, upon closer examination we see as not at all different from ourselves. In an increasingly mongrelized, multi-social and cultural world that is cooking up new permutations biologically, emotionally, and spiritually, we are waking up to the magnificence and inclusiveness of a an embracing ethos of love and community; hybrid spirits seeking the same things – happiness, peace, love, and especially belonging. And in moving forward together with such a vision, we bring closer to reality the possibility of a sustainable Ecology of Oneness.

The forces behind the growth of such a vision and the methods we can embrace to "become the change we wish to see in the world" are the heart, soul, backbone, and reason for what follows.

Chapter Two

The Bigger Story:

The State We Are In

Not that long ago in terms of human history, we were the center of it all. The wise ones who we looked to for guidance and to help us know our place in the scheme of things told us that we lived on the surface of a big flat landmass around and above which all stars, even our sun revolved. Not only that, but of all the many creatures created by the One (sometimes She, but more recently He) who made everything, we were at the top of the heap, especially the men.

This may not have been the ubiquitous view of all the wise men and women of the planet. But it was for the wise men whose ancestors most of us here in the West trace our roots from.

For some with nostalgic inclinations, it was a simpler time. This does not mean that the indomitable human spirit did not seek the edges, to grow in understanding of the natural world through contemplation, calculation, and invented instrumentation to help us stretch out senses further and further. Alas, curiosity and revelations of a new order were often met with house arrest, banishment, beheadings, and burnings at the stake, curbing the enthusiasm to embrace new discoveries and revelations pointing to a different version of the world and our place – at least for a while.

At any given point in time, as we sort out what needs to be done and what works in the circumstances we find ourselves in, we come to assumptive agreements with those around us so that we are all, more or less, on the same page. The ordinary, daily stuff of life then begins to have a life of its own in the customs, codes, and laws that we all agree to abide by. This is what is known as reification. Of course, wanting this to fit into a grander scheme of things, we then ratchet up our reasons or justifications for why things are this way through the process of deification, which, as the word implies, can also be how we perceive or conceive of a higher power or grand architect of it all. These two processes, reification and deification are the natural social, psychological, and metaphysical/theological processes by which we construct a reality. This constructed version of the world usually makes sense at first. But time marches on. Circumstances change. Needs change. But more often than not, as creatures of habit, an important issue that we shall address later on, with our heads more firmly rooted in what was than what is, knowledge and assumptions around that knowledge gleaned from the past remain in place for a longer time than is useful. This is especially true when the meaning makers and power brokers in our societies have *self* more in mind than *other*, and find it hard to let go of their grip and the benefits they reap until they can, with any luck, eliminate the competition and grab onto whatever new paradigm that is arising. Such is the history of aristocracies, warlords, castes, worldly and theocratic potentates, and the institutions whose glove their hand has slipped into. And if new players manage to come onto the scene, sooner or later, they too learn to master the processes of reification and deification machinations to suit a new "age" or era, which is possibly more enlightened - but possibly not.

In the case of our central position on the stage at the center of the universe, although there were the geniuses of earlier days like Copernicus and Galileo, who saw the fallacy of this view, the ongoing march and onslaught of science and technology cannot but damage and eventually destroy this fairy tale disguised as spiritual doctrine and dogma. And despite the efforts of fundamentalist interests to periodically prop us up to our previous undisputed lofty heights, the dissemination of TMI (aka "too much information") gone into the hands of too many has forever toppled us from our perch.

Still, to this day, a struggle between rational and irrational worldviews compete for the hearts and minds of those who wish it was all just so much easier than what we are facing right now. In the West, we possibly struggle more because our "fall from grace" has come with a theology where a good deal of emphasis is placed on embodiment guilt and the fear of displeasing a omniscient, omnipotent, omnipresent Creator. I remember hearing supposedly intelligent and rational people claim that 9/11 was the result of our government allowing abortions and that Hurricane Katrina was because of our tolerance of homosexuals. Why else would God betray us, making us, as A.E. Housman laments, "stranger(s) and afraid in a world we never made." The only way to keep us rooted in a worldview and the philosophies and theologies of a time before the great discoveries of the

Renaissance and after is to create or reinforce with greater zeal the forces of sin, guilt, and a need for repentance – to suggest that despite our fall from being the center of it all, if we only embrace God, Jesus, Mohammed, this or that Guru we shall, in the light and grace of their being, find our rightful place. It is the promise of paradise, of the "Good News."

The problem with such an approach at this point is that we have gone way beyond the point at which a rational and mature understanding of who, what, and where we are in it all will allow. And even if all of the information contradicting or challenging these fundamentalist claims is not complete, the force and intensity of such faiths to exclude, ban, or shun such knowledge deconstructs in their own maniacal attempts to hold back the information tide unending.

At the same time, I would contend that even those who claim to be progressive and humanistic struggle just as much with the amazing, mind-boggling information that science and technology is bringing forth that similarly demands of them to reframe many of the existential questions and claims they use for their own reasons for being and place in the universe. Even if one is an agnostic or atheist, the realities revealed through quantum physics and the ever-deepening physical sciences, which discover layer upon layer of mathematic harmonies and geometric perfection leave one wondering about authorship and orchestration. Thus, it really comes as no surprise that in the face of what he had discovered in terms of the fabric of the universe, Einstein became more convinced in the existence of a god (but not necessarily the same endorsed by his Christian or Jewish friends).

Our Place in the Universe

Science now observes that the immensity of the known universe beyond which many believers of Western faiths believe is the heaven of God, is expanding. This expansion is happening at a rate wherein – based on current scientific thinking – the universe will double in size in 11.4 billion years. This may seem an awfully long time, unless you consider that the visible universe is estimated to be **20 billion light years in diameter**. So, our universe keeps seizing heavenly real estate, forcing the God "upstairs" to re-locate.

Priests and elders of time past had no idea what size the universe was or the number of stars in the sky. All they "knew" is that it all revolved around our flat planet. Then with telescopes, astrolabes, and the daring of stargazers, seamen, and physicists we discovered that our planet was round and the only reason we did not fall off was because of a force known as gravity. Not only that, but as our knowledge of our physical world has continued to this day, we now know that day and night arise because our planet spins on its axis once every 24 hours at the rate of **1038 miles per hour (mph)** while zooming around the sun every 365 days at the speed of **60,000mph** and that our solar system with the sun in the center and the other planets that revolve around it of which we are just one revolves around the center our galaxy, the Milky Way **every 200 million years at the speed of 406,800mph** whilst our galaxy is similarly racing through space in an ever expanding universe along with the other estimated **100 billion galaxies**; galaxies that are not that different from our own. Does it make sense that all of these other galaxies would be dead or have no human-like or even human life like our own? Are we that special for God to create such a vast universe with nothing at all like us anywhere else? In a world of such mathematical precision and elegance I would consider it a waste of space if there weren't at least a few other creatures like us out there somewhere.

While you may be able to answer the questions, "Where were you born?" or "Where do you come from?" even "Where are you now?" in the bigger scheme of things you are NEVER in the same place twice from one moment to the next. Your sense of place, where you come from, where your roots are only conventions that may help us feel more grounded, but are – in fact – wholly fictitious. I spoke earlier of valuing the places from which you came. But, in the grander scheme of the physical universe, this place is only relatively useful within the context of the narrative of our lives – which – I am sorry to say – I shall similarly deconstruct shortly.

To make matters worse, even if you were to claim your turf as something solid and real, something that you can always count on, it is just not so. Gaia, the pagan name for Mother Earth, has always been churning and throbbing, cooking and cooling, rocking and rolling. She does so as a living, pulsating inter-dependent entity of a solar system racing through space on the spiral wings of the Milky Way, visiting and passing her through the gravitational fields and more physical hazards of meteors, comets and the like. With all this movement and commotion, landmasses have emerged from or re-submerged into primordial oceans. Continents have come together, split apart and re-shaped themselves time and time again. Meteors have crashed into them and countless earthquakes and volcanoes have cracked and re-defined terrains, increasing and decreasing land masses precipitating changes of tides and weather patterns – regardless of whether you want to ascribe any of these phenomena or changes in their patterns to human activity and/or consumption. Hurricanes, tornadoes, droughts, floods, earthquakes, volcanoes, tsunamis, even Ice Ages; these are every bit a part of our earthly realm as a pleasant sunny day by the beach. And, the life forms living on the skin of Gaia just have to put up with it and figure out where and how to be safe – for the time being – and carry on doing whatever our body-mind feels compelled or inspired to do. To wish for sunny beaches every day and to ascribe anything adverse to our human whims as something we or someone else is to blame for is both infantile and arrogant. This does not mean that I am not a believer in global warming or that our current human activity is not having its adverse effect. It just means that regardless of how safe or mindful we play it, like every other species on the planet, our human body-mind will have to contend with these forces and facts regardless. But, if we know how to not make it worse, it is probably not a bad idea to make efforts in that direction. Otherwise, it is like jumping out of a plane with a sack of rocks on your back rather than a parachute.

Biological Facts

In a world and universe that bespeaks change as the only constant, a world of impermanence, we cannot ignore nor deny the science that, similarly, points to forces and process within what we call our physical being that shouts impermanence.

What is the nature of this very body and mind upon and in which we construct an ego and a sense of "me"-ness? In answering these questions, we must always be aware of the backdrop of four irrefutable facts about this body and mind formation. We are born. We age. We get sick. We die.

In a moment of what we hope was inspiring we are conceived. An egg unites with a visiting sperm and the spark at the center of a nascent being is lit. This is human life at its most basic. Any arguments that debate the fact as to when human life begins are theological and philosophical gymnastics to justify one position or another; i.e. human contrivance to make us feel better about our positions and decisions. Abortion is killing. But, then again, for us to live, killing is what happens from the moment we are conceived. Both animal and plant life is sacrificed constantly through our entire life cycle to support our existence. We should never forget this. And if, we do, we lead an ungrateful life, which has its own consequences. Choices are made along the way. How conscious and mindful are we?

But, back to the real story.

From this sperm and egg event there evolves a human form that will have anywhere between **100 to 1400 trillion cells** by the time we are full grown adults.

And in the daily growth and body-mind evolution we go through along the way, there will be an estimated **50 to 70 billion cells that will die each day**. It is said that your entire **blood supply is changed out every 21 days** and that **within 7 years, whatever you identify as you in the mirror is gone, gone, gone**. If you rule out growing and aging and are looking just as smashing as you did seven years before, the fact is that the you who stand there now was not standing there then.

We look in the mirror and see a solid form. But, if we press here or there, we are varying degrees of squishy – with our head (no surprise here) being the hardest. That squishiness bespeaks a body that is more liquid than solid. In fact, we are approximately seventy percent water, leaving only thirty percent being what makes us solid. Being made up of so much water, does it not make sense that like the oceans and waterways that similarly make up seventy percent of our planet (Are we the microcosm of a macrocosm as oriental medicine teaches?) that our moods and energy levels are affected by the moon (which, by the way is **traveling at 2,210mph around the earth**) and shifting gravitational influences? Consider that there are more conceptions and that labor cycles around the full moon, and that emergency rooms are filled with fight victims and mental hospitals have historically deployed more straight jackets during that time.

But what is even more remarkable is that regardless of whether the cells in our body are more water-like or solid, **each of these cells is made of atoms**. Atoms are made of small units; protons, neutrons, electrons and so on. With respect to scale, these particles are a considerable distance from each other. That is, most of what atoms are is space.

Thus, the greatest volume that fills the human package that we inhabit **is mostly space**. And through this space, there is a force of attraction and repulsion which holds each and every atom in each and every cell, in each and every organ and tissue together. Positive and negative charges, yin and yang, yab and yum, yoni and lingum, Adam and Eve, Shakti and Shiva; male and female in balance, inter-dependent, vibrating. In truth, **we are space beings vibrating with energy**.

As vibrational beings whose very existence is dependent upon the polarity of positive and negative electro-magnetic influences at the most basic level, would it not be common sense or logical for us to perceive, know, and possibly accept that our psyches and soma are effected by gravity, phases of the moon, tides, electrical storms and other larger weather phenomena, sunspots, the electro-magnetic pulsations of planets and stars, and the staggering speeds beyond light that we travel through the universe? This IS our natural world; a world whose influence and impact is measured and predicted in both the natural and occult sciences. Astro- and quantum physics verify and quantify the impact of subtle forces that shamans and astrologers felt and observed in the moods and behaviors of animal, plant, and human life. The human instrument, so often dulled by our modern living, is vindicated as genuine and useful as we develop the tools and instruments that stretch the capabilities of our senses into realms so many of us never knew were there.

But, what about the energetic and vibrational world we have created for ourselves? What about microwaves, microwave towers, and Bluetooth devices stuck to the sides of our heads? We may try to deny these three because we like our microwaved popcorn and can't get enough of our cell-phone technology. But in the not-so-distant past we learned of the dangerous effects of the "invisible" forces of x-ray exposure and witnessed or could not deny what nuclear radiation does to human atoms, cells, and tissues.

The most basic substances that keep us alive in this vibrational body made up of the natural elements are air, water, and food – in that order. Without air, we are gone within a few minutes. With water, a few days. With food, our languishing varies depending on our body types, our strengths and so on. It is said that there are people who do not need to eat; who can exist on sunlight alone. While this is wonderful in a theoretical kind of way, most of us will gradually move towards death as the normal workings of our digestive system shut down. These three substances, air, water, and food bind us together; in fact, makes us inter-dependent and inseparable. Here we focus on air and water.

Consider the fact that the breath you take in still contains molecules breathed out by Julius Caesar, Mahatma Gandhi, the granny next door, and her dog. The air of this planet flows in, around, and through us. We share the air and in it are contained atoms, molecules, and cells that have been impacted by other places and the cellular memories of countless others.   There are many traditions that encourage spiritual aspirants to go on solitary retreats. And, when I have met such men and women, they seem to be more embodied, more of themselves. Many of their practices focus on energetically preserving and embellishing that awareness. The greatest masters are those who have mastered themselves and learned to be in the world without being thrown this way and that from the vibrations of others. Is this ability, at its most basic, the fact that for a concentrated time these men and women were breathing mostly and learned to master their own breath? Would this not explain the importance that martial arts, the yogic sciences, and meditation teachings place on the mastery and attention to the breath? Even then, that we master this in no way makes us any less inter-dependent and connected to the breath that we all inevitably breathe.

With respect to water and our life, the inter-dependent charges in our vibration have created bodies that exhibit more water and watery than solid qualities. This is probably why it is so natural for us to refer to the flow of our life, a smooth flow of communication between ourselves and others, and so on. Like air, the water that is in us, has been around us, and quite possibly through many other life forms along the way. In jest but possibly because they know that sewer and water treatment systems inevitably feed back into the taps whose water is boiled for tea, some irreverent British refer to the water from their taps as "Her Majesty's urine." The ebb and flow of waters through us are inextricably connected to and often just the same as the waters that flow around us.

Thus, when it comes to air and water, does it not also make perfect sense that as humans on this planet, it is preposterous if not suicidal if we allow our air and water supplies to be polluted or in the case of water, depleted? Similarly, should we not judiciously manage the vibrational influences of the invisible electro-magnetic and radioactive products and by-products that we create? Does it make sense for us to allow politicians and corporate moguls of energy sources more concerned with financial return and dominance to make decisions over such fundamental aspects of our lives over and above the wisdom of scientists and environmentalists?

Our Mortal March

Even if we were not being threatened from without by natural or man-made means, our biological being – nonetheless – has its own time clock. The twinkle that we once were in our father's eye, that spark that has persisted in the daily presence of our body and mind continues to move and morph within itself. It does this with or without ease or difficulty depending on a myriad of factors which can be summed up by our circumstances, how well we learn to nurture this body-mind to keep the electro-magnetic polarity of our cells firing efficiently, and our emotions. But regardless of whether or not we live in a palace or dumpster, whether we eat raw vegan organic tidbits or Twinkies and bologna, and whether we are endlessly optimistic or horribly depressed, it will all be over in the blink of an eye; certainly in a very short time compared to the age of our planet, solar system, galaxy, and universe.

It is said that change is the only constant. With respect to our physical universe, we see from what has been presented thus far that there is absolutely no thing that is permanent or stays the same in the same place. All is change. All is in flux. Here today, gone much faster than tomorrow in actuality. But, is it just denial of the truth of impermanence that leads us to crave stability, permanence, peace, and with them, happiness? Or, could it be that where we look to find happiness, in all that is impermanent, is just the wrong place to look?

The world's great philosophies and wisdom traditions do their best to explain to us that we are looking for happiness and – yes – love in all the wrong places. Jesus said that the Kingdom of Heaven is found within. The Buddha spoke of our Buddhanature. The concepts of soul in so many traditions always encourage us to look within, to find that the satisfaction, the grounding, the love we seek must be discovered from within for there to be any quality of a lasting vision of it in our everyday world. Thus, the stability, the sense of who we really are, the home we are looking for IS real. But, it is found between our ears and in our heart. The ephemeral comfort we find in the world is a reflection of this awareness. To rely on the "picture in the mirror" and lose sight of what allowed it to arise in the first place, is to fall asleep and/or become mesmerized by a phantasm of that which is nothing more than a temporary – albeit illusory - respite, something not worth banking on in the long run.

To wake up to this realization takes work and we tend to only work when we are pushed or confronted. We usually try to hold onto whatever we think is out there, our reified world, that we erroneously define as the cause of our happiness, our bliss. But even if what we are trying to hold onto is unraveling before our very eyes, we cling tight. Unaware, unprepared or unwilling to take the "real" plunge, to really let go of the reified world, we persist in a dualistic story that lays out the landscape of our material world and all therein contained. And, with others who feel in the same dilemma with whom we have a bond or connection, we construct a "sacred" world that exemplifies all the answers to all the quandaries we face in our day-to-day world. We have no place in the physical world where there is not change and upheaval. So the sacred world of heaven is permanent, reliable, and peaceful; a guaranteed solid place to be for those who believe. Free of birth, old age, sickness, and death, in this heaven we remain free of disease, "Forever 21," happy and at peace. And rather than deal with our nagging parents, spouses, and self-serving leaders and masters, there is one – or maybe several- masters (gods, goddesses, ascended masters and the like) who righteously and/or lovingly preside over us – all the time and forever more.

I don't think there is anyone alive who would not want to believe and/or maybe live in a utopia free of sickness, poverty, and warfare, replete with nice people and super beings to keep it all humming blissfully. And maybe it does – in fact – exist. But, what makes the reality of such a heavenly realm and its occupants questionable is that there are so many variations and interpretations of what this looks like, what the rules or prerequisites are to get in, i.e. who is eligible or "chosen," who is excluded, and so on.

In days gone by, when the reality of the five-mile radius circumscribing our lives was more the norm than the exception, the sanctity of our group's version would have worked to "hold down the fort" for a while. But, not anymore. This is not our world. And in virtually every corner of the world, the many factors I have laid out thus far and shall expand upon in what follows have contributed to us probably never being able to reclaim such. Unlike Dr. Seuss's returning hatted cat, this cat is out of the bag and has no intention of going back.

Coming Apart at The Seams

I once saw on the billboard of a church, "This is the past that someone in the future is longing to go back to." We always assume that the days of the past were simpler. It is hard to know if this is true or not because we are using our present-day brain to assess what less or simpler is. Perhaps even cavemen had their daily dilemmas and existential crises, conflicts with their kids and arguments with their spouses, and the annoyance of the guy in the cave next store who kept making and banging on drums. We see that when we are vexed or in any particular mood, we can color the world that way. In a world constructed by a mind that doesn't understand, gets attached to its own views and perceptions, and resists the views or thoughts of others to the contrary, what the Buddhists call the Three Poisons of ignorance, attachment, and aggression, none of this has real possibility of changing. Thus, it is probably a false assumption to bemoan our lives as more complicated than the cave people. However, the bits of information about our world and where it comes from IS vastly different from our ancestors from even fifty or sixty years ago. And, I contend, this does make a difference.

The rapid and almost daily scientific revelations about our circumstances on this vibrating, pulsing, life-giving spaceship we call earth in relation to the universe and the empty, space-nature of our veritable human form were beyond our senses, capabilities, and reasoning for a good part of our development as a species and the civilizations we spawned along the way. Perhaps the people of Lemuria or Atlantis had it all figured out - or at least some of it - and knew these facts of life. But, with only vestiges, hearsay, and fragmented records to go on, what we understand about our world until relatively recent times, relied upon the meaning and purpose - the reified and deified worlds - we derived from our experiences of the land, its flora, fauna and other members of our tribes or clans within a five mile radius of where we were born. Not just some protoplasmic blobs, we used our sensitivities and intelligence to figure out how we could best survive and perhaps manage a world we certainly knew was changing. Night and day, weather events, the seasons, our own progression from birth to death - all gave us a sense of sensibility and rhythm. As mentioned before, from all this we developed codes and cultural agreements between those we lived with to negotiate through time and what it tended to - within a usual set of parameters - present us. Certain behaviors and lines of reasoning were in line with what most could or were willing to live with and by. To make these codes and agreements more special, we elevated them to the special status of being sacred. This sacredness was mediated by those who ruled the realms of the sacred. Perhaps if those were truly wise or enlightened people, the rules and codes made reflected their awareness and allowed for there to be flexibility and openness in the natural progression of events over time. Nevertheless, those who didn't like or abide by the codes and agreements that the many agreed to risked being labeled as outlaws, outcasts, mad, sinners, and possibly even a danger to the peace and tranquility that "we" sought in "our place" with "our people." To not follow what was reified and pay homage to what was deified was to risk chaos, death, and destruction. Thus the lawbreakers or non-believers needed to be ignored, shunned, banned, cast out, converted, or put to death. Keep in mind that we are not talking here about those who do harmful things to others, such as beat, abuse, kill, or so forth. Here I am speaking of those who just saw things a different way.

Thus people in agreement on a number of levels and beyond family units established clans, tribes, communities with a more homogenous culture of customs and beliefs. Customs, the desire to cooperate, and a shared belief in what was absolute and absolutely necessary for the healthy growth and happiness of the community bound people together. Of course, human experience is not so uniform as to not cause variation in minds and hearts. There would people that are more compliant, more parochial, than others. Thus there would be the town or village sheriff, doctor, priest, clown, busybody, idiot, and rebel: the movers, shakers, and the troublemakers and so on. But who took what part in the communal drama would change and change again. Laws and rules would become outmoded. There would be staunch conservatives and heretics or progressives. Battles would ensue on various levels to change or keep things the same. Such is human life. But, all of these changes would still be experienced and worked out in the context and continuum of people who had historical, genetic, and ecological ties to each other.

But, it is part of human nature to want to know what is on and over the horizon. And there would be those whose itch for adventure and change could only be scratched by stepping beyond the five-mile mark. And when or if they returned, they returned with a different perspective based on new information and experiences. Initially welcomed back, so often the sojourners would feel and/or find themselves held as different, perhaps even rejected. Thus the archetypes of the hermits, the recluses, the ones who live on the edge of the forest, in the mountains; the mysterious ones with funny ideas.

There were places of commerce and pilgrimage where people from various places met to exchange things and ideas. Cities were especially dangerous, not necessarily because they were dangerous, but because one would encounter people whose culture, customs, and beliefs were different from those held in your hometown. Absolutes about the world became relativized. Revealed as just human constructs, how could you return to your village and listen to someone tell you that if you thought, said, or did this or that, that you risked alienation, madness, hellfire, or damnation? More than a lost soul, you risked being viewed as a threat to the entire village.

If a village could not trivialize, successfully demean, contain, quell or burn at the stake unwanted influences and the ones who brought them, the infection of possibility or a more relative view would spread. And if more people left to experience the same and returned, the infection could become an epidemic, ravaging an entire way of life – or so would be the thinking of those incapable or unwilling to accept the change that was upon them.

Although an idealization of the village life of yesteryear, the historical data of a world prior to the Industrial Revolution paints a picture similar to the one I describe. And while there have been variations and times more enlightened and/or progressive than others that came and went, the infection of relativity destroying absolutist views of the world held by clans, tribes, and villages has exploded exponentially.

We once could perhaps walk from one village to the next. With horses, camels and other carrier beast of burden we could go over the mountain. Boats got us down stream and across waterways to new continents. Trains and cars have helped us to cross entire continents. And air travel has made all of this that much quicker where we can be in LA at dinnertime and be in London for lunch the next day.

With borders dissolving and easier access to more places, in any given day we may see men in suits, smocks, tunics, holy robes, djellabas, and loin clothes, sporting fezzes, yarmulkes, turbans, bowler hats, or hoodies. Women may be in suits, dresses, saris, hula skirts, or burkas. As the goods, wares, and fare of the different people and their customs move around the planet, we become acquainted with and possibly even prefer the food, clothing, music, and art of another or many lands and their people. And with Amazon, just go online, "click," and whatever you fancy can be at your doorstep tomorrow.

Then, if we open our mouths and hearts, if we begin to understand another language and read what others read, we find ourselves encountering some people who believe just as strongly as we might in one God who has a covenant with and loves them above all others. Or, people with many gods who have different jobs and care for everyone. Or, people with no god in particular, but study with teachers or priests who encourage them to connect with and care for others, irrespective of their beliefs.

Theists, atheists, agnostics, humanists, nihilists – all bumping in to each other, sharing food, clothes, ideas, affections, making friends, making babies, creating possibility, creating new levels of uncertainty and confusion...on and on to the point where, in your neighborhood, there may be ten churches of various denominations and sects, a synagogue, a mosque, and meditation center, each passively or in no uncertain terms wanting you to know that their path or divine hero would like you to join them. The absolute assumptions you may have thought you shared with your neighbor no longer exist – if – upon closer examination - they ever really existed in the first place.

Add to this invasion of heathens, non-believers, damned, and other others, there is mass media.

In the party game of Chinese whispers, one person says a word or phrase and then it is observed whether that word or phrase remains the same as it is whispered around a circle. More often than not, the word or phrase gets spun based on how we hear and interpret what the person whispering to us has said.

Despite the fact that we know very well how even this simple game of communications can go awry, as social beings who value how much more easily our lives go when we cooperate, we have spent millennium trying to connect with others though words, sounds, and visions; oral teachings, written word, radio, television, and the internet. Even if you were to shut the doors and try to home school your children with only your voice and opinion and the written opinions of your selected few, unless you make sure that they never hear a radio, turn on a television, or connect to the internet, the infection of relativization will infect your home via invisible bands of wavelengths.

So Who Are We in These Days and What are the Consequences?

In an ever-expanding Free World of ideas, ideologies, cultures, and commodities, there is a growing number of human beings who have a better understanding of the fragile and ephemeral nature of our existence. Maybe you did not know, but now you do, that we breathe air and drink water that is cycled and recycled through us from time immemorial. We eat foods from around the world that have supported other body structures in other climes, but now build our bodies as well. We experience the emotion and spiritual consequences of customs and beliefs foreign to our own that demand from us to be more open and tolerant if we are to not only survive, but thrive. And we are in a world where there are many religious, economic, and political forces that wish we knew none of this.

We are at an interesting point in history. The vastly increased information and knowledge pointing us squarely at the truth of our physical, biological, and social worlds has brought more poignantly into question who we are, what we are in relation to it all, and what – if anything – to believe or hold onto as some kind of permanent reference point to give our lives meaning beyond merely existing. This has no doubt been one of humanity's eternal quests as change is the constant that we have been reeling from since we had conscious awareness to do so. And we have created and utilized spiritual tools and religious systems to make us – at least – feel more comfortable, which I think is a necessary component of the process as the late great blues man, Willie Dixon, understood when he sang, "I'm built for comfort. I ain't built for speed." But claim as they will or try as they might, none of the world's wisdom traditions or paradigms seem to have all of the answers. They would like to. And, in the past, they may have – or so it was thought. But, because each one of these systems has addressed the big questions that eat at us from within, some of the answers they provide are of value. And, I contend that if the priests and other absolute meaning makers can allow their tradition or message to offer their wisdom in a free market in a free world, then they will continue to have relevance in modern, chaotic, cosmopolitan life.

In the end, the answers to the questions we ask can be reduced to a simple directive. We want peace. We want stability. But, above all, we want to be happy. Oddly or not so oddly enough, the truth is that deep down, we do <u>know</u> what creates these three: LOVE. That we have been looking for LOVE in all the wrong places, in places and spaces within and around us that are transient at best, does not mean that LOVE is an illusion or delusion; that it is hopelessly out of reach. If that were so, we would not pursue it. But, deep down, we can feel it. More than anything else, it is who we are. While we in the west are more use to the idea of we humans being "sinners," the traditions of the East, especially the mind science of Buddhism posits that at our core, we are "basically good." In my book, *The Passionate Buddha*, I go one step further and say that this basic goodness is our **inherent loving nature**. And that is what I wish to address in the chapters that follow.

As shall be revealed in subsequent chapters, the Ecology of Oneness, is based on the knowledge that LOVE is who we are. It calls upon eclectically minded, critically thinking individuals to wake up to the light within them. In a world where sickness, poverty, and warfare spiral out of control from greed and self-interest, a deeper, more ecological and all inclusive viewpoint is the only viable solution.

Before addressing this ecological viewpoint, I first feel compelled to offer my observations on the spiritual and religious milieu of our times.

Chapter Three

The Quandaries and Quagmires of Belief

Although suffering in its various guises still dominates the movie box offices and daytime television, I almost think it prophetic that Pharrell Williams' "Happy" became such a worldwide phenomenon. Despite the many challenges we face, there are still shards of light pointing to better days.

So I repeat myself when I say that we all want to be happy. We certainly would prefer not to suffer. And, once we have a situation where our basic human survival needs of food, water, clothing, and shelter are met and there is a modicum of happy greater than sad, then perhaps we have enough mental real estate available to begin to ask the bigger questions of who we are and what this world we are in is about. Regardless of whether we practice a religion or not, issues of happiness, suffering, and meaning are what our human hearts and brains strive to attain, avoid, and comprehend respectively. And it makes sense that as a social institution, religion makes these basics central to doctrine, practice and dogma. While it can be agreed that these are what creates a commonality amongst religions, in an ever-changing world in which these needs and wants are not always stable or satisfied, how these are attained and how the means to attain them are justified, reified, and deified lead to competition, conflict, even war. So, whilst the needs and possibly even the logic, practices, and justifications are not dissimilar in theory and the intentions initially noble or sincere, how religions are practiced and used as justification for ensuring that its members are taken care of first and foremost and above all others has, historically, been problematic.

It is not an uncommon adage of people who are considered or define themselves as being progressive or open minded to say in some form of politically correct speak, that, really – in truth – all religions or spiritual paths lead to the same goal. All paths are merely going up different sides of the great mountain that we humans traverse to reach the summit and whatever awaits us there.

While I do believe that all of us – humans and other creatures of creation alike – seek happiness and want to control as many factors as we can to ensure an ongoing going flow of continuously happy moments, beyond this very visceral, tangible, shared wish, I cannot accept this adage beyond it being a social platitude that sounds wise and tolerant in certain company.

My first issue with it is that it assumes that religion and spirituality are one in the same thing, if not interchangeable; that if you speak of someone as being spiritual, it is most often implied that they are a serious practitioner of one religion or another. However, I have met as many – if not more – spiritually oriented folk who profess no religion as those who do. An interesting factoid from the annals of Wikipedia is that in these days, when people refer to themselves as being spiritual, they are often trying to explain the fact that despite them not practicing a dominant or known religion – mainly a Judeo-Christian one – they still do things like yoga, tai chi, practice mediation, follow a guru or whatever other spiritual "things." But even if we speak of these notions, religion and spirituality, with the same institution, we are confronted by the distinction where some follow the letter of the "law," - the

exoteric rules and regulations which identify them to everyone else as members of that institution, and those who follow the "spirit" of the law, the *esoteric* or implicit understanding and practices that lead one to "feel" that they are part of the institution, regardless of what others perceive.

Whereas spirituality is defined by modern social scientists as a search for what is sacred and/or worth venerating over and above the ordinary conventions of the culture or times in which we live (what I ascribe to being more of the esoteric side of a religion), religion per se is a socially constructed body of beliefs or assumptions one can ascribe to or more than likely be born into, hence explicitly exoteric. While it is assumed that the raison d'etre of religion is the spiritual search, if it is truly to function as such, it should serve, not define or circumscribe the spiritual search. However, the fact that it serves social, cultural, and political functions as well does at times bypass or run roughshod over the existential and absolute questions and issues that it professes to answer and/or embody.

Furthermore, this adage assumes or there is a tacit agreement being sought from those saying such that while there may indeed be some bickering now and then between those who profess whatever religion they profess, that others from different faiths share the same message as the message professed by our own faith. That is, in plain speak: "We are bickering (or fighting) because you don't understand that your point of view is really the same as my point of view. You just don't see it yet." Too often in ecumenical meetings and circles I have heard this unexamined platitude which more often than not only refers to the world's "great" religions – (in alphabetical order so as to show no bias) Christianity, Hinduism, Islam, and Judaism, and whilst not really a religion and not theistically centered, Buddhism. More than likely when being uttered it does not take into account those practicing as Wiccan, Druids, Satan worshippers, or the faiths and religious practices of millions of indigenous people around the globe.

At best, this seemingly benign utterance with its simplistic assumptions is an attempt to counterbalance the history and legacy of religions professing that whoever their followers and faithful are, they are the "Chosen People, " leaving all others out in the cold at best – but more than likely unsaved, uncivilized, and probably headed into a fiery abyss when the time comes for them to leave this earthly abode.

Of course, if you are intelligent and modern, you may think that such thoughts are not a part of the religious thought or practices of people today. But, in recent years at a prestigious American university with young people who represent the leaders of our future, there was an ecumenical meeting sponsored by a charismatic Christian group that I was invited to attend. It was a Friday night and I thought that an ecumenical program would perhaps draw ten kids. The rest would be out getting drunk or having sex, or both, like the good old days. But, to my shock (and somewhat horror) the meeting attracted about eight hundred students, what the organizers expected (again, shock). Over the course of the proceedings I came to fully understand that this was not really an ecumenical meeting; where people of different faiths could compare and contrast views, expand awareness and appreciation. This was a gathering so that young faithful could see who their enemies were. On stage sat a rabbi, a Muslim professor, a local well-revered

Christian author popular to the sponsoring organization, and myself, a Buddhist.

The line of questioning from the audience seemed staged. And in this

orchestrated atmosphere, I watched a young neophyte take a microphone in a

packed auditorium and ask the Muslim professor if he would accept Jesus Christ as

his savior. Without skipping a beat, the professor fired back at this neophyte and

the entire audience that unless the Koran was chanted to them at the time of their

death, they would all go to hell anyway.

Again, a major prestigious university of educated people. In their own eyes,

chosen.

Chosen People

Chosen people. This has been a big problem on this planet. Reifying our beliefs

and asserting an absolutist certainty of those beliefs with ourselves having a special

relationship with them and the being or central figure we claim to give us that

authority or acclaim, becomes the passport to do unto others and the planet what

we see fit with sanctions from that which is beyond question. Tribes of the Middle

East and elsewhere decimating those whose lands and stuff they think "God" wants

them to have, the crusades, the Spanish Inquisition, witch burnings, pogroms,

Manifest Destiny, the holocaust, the rationale behind jihad and honor killings, and

the slaughter or subjugation of millions of peoples around the world. Sometimes

such acts have been done in the name of religion to presumably protect the "fold"

and root out infidels and apostates. More often than not, however, the religious reasoning has been mere justification used by nations and/or corporations for land and resource acquisition. As a Chosen People, you can get away with murder, and even more.

Zealots, xenophobes, people who claim to be chosen or think that they have an inside track with a Supreme Being all share one thing in common; an external reference point. Guided by dogma and dictates or educated in a dualistic way that fosters adherence to experts, authorities, and external markers as indicative of achievement and worth, individuals and organizations that foster such value memorization and compliance over the development of critical thinking skills and discourage self-awareness. The result is a populace that can adhere to and even become fanatical about what is right and wrong, what or who is good and what or who is bad. In a dualistic, black and white world, the ambiguity of reality is not a call to pause or reflect, but rather to censor or expunge. Those who do not follow your doctrine should perhaps be tolerated. But they are best converted, exiled, or obliterated.

With an external reference point for morality and action, whether it is in the name of a cause or God, you can literally get away with and justify almost – if not entirely – everything. You are only following orders or God's will. Or perhaps you are "saved," which means from this point on, it really doesn't matter what havoc you wreak on the world, your loved ones, or anyone else who gets in your way or your desires.

This does not mean that there is no place for dogma or dictums for those who would otherwise harm themselves or others. I am okay where the fear or wrath of

God is enough to stop one from committing murder, rape, or the like. But, at some point in the spiritual unfoldment of each and every one of us, we must wake up to the awareness of our own abilities to turn to our own hearts for guidance. For anyone to claim to be doing God's will – no matter who they are – is presumptuous, absurd, if not potentially dangerous. In fact, history has borne out that it IS dangerous.

Although the historical record in the West would verify that the three major religions of the west, Christianity, Islam, and Judaism, have overtly or covertly been responsible for or been the legitimizing or sanctioning doctrine justifying more deaths and acts like the above more than any other group in recent centuries, this does not mean that other peoples and traditions have not done similar things, although perhaps not to the same scale. No doubt others in the course of history with absolutist or special insider claims have justified taking over a village, decimating a rival clan or family. And, not too dissimilar to the various expressions of Chosen people "fever" that spawned debate, dissention, and war in the history of Western civilization, the same antics pepper the history of the East as well.

In fact, the backdrop to the life of a wealthy and powerful prince, Siddhartha Gautama, who was to become known as Sakyamuni Buddha – who most of us call "the Buddha" (despite the fact that according Buddhist history he was the fourth historical Buddha) – was a time when many teachers and the cultures and nations they were a part of believed fervently that their ideas about and practices to supplicate, worship, and connect with a Supreme Being were the best, if not the only ones that should be practiced or allowed. There is a tradition in the East where the heads of two or more spiritual schools would engage in open debate and whoever the aristocrats and learned judges deemed superior in their reasoning and rationale for their celestial paradigm would not only be declared the victor, but all the other teachers in the debate and their students would then follow the victor's way. But this noble and seemingly fair process was not necessarily always the only way ecclesiastic superiority was established. Intrigue, assassinations, warfare were also some of the cards on the table. In the case of Sakyamuni, his view that everyone possessed awakening potential, i.e. Buddhanature challenged the caste system supported by Hindu orthodoxy and was met with violence. Consequently, some of the Buddha's disciples fled to the West. But, these attacks also backfired, leading to the growth of those wishing to follow the Buddha's teachings.

In the story of the awakening of Siddhartha Gautama to his spiritual destiny, we learn that not only did he engage in the practice of meditation. He used the depth of insight gleaned to sharpen his abilities to concentrate, contemplate, and develop various qualities of wisdom, including the ability to discriminate without bias. A spiritual aspirant, he was still a prince who knew well the games of nobility in nation building and the role and reasoning behind military conquest and the use of religion as justification and dispensation for waging wars. Reflecting on the heated debates on the nature and being of Brahma, the Supreme Being of the Hindu tradition of his native India, Siddhartha raised a simple question: If there is an absolute version of who and what Brahma is, then we should all be in agreement. After all, that is what absolutes are. Consequently, if we are in disagreement about those absolutes, then whatever we say must somehow be tainted with one form of bias or another. Thus we are no longer talking about absolutes, but <u>relative</u> perceptions about those absolutes. Our perceptions, our version is just our version, based on our own particular life experiences and the conclusions we have drawn. They are tempered by our upbringing, our environment, our mental capacities, our emotional tendencies, and the circumstances that life presents us. Therefore, he concluded, if we really want to know the absolute truth, if we really want to know Brahma/God, then we first have to examine how the assumptions we make based on our experiences color what we see and come to "know."

Siddhartha embarked on his own path to examine his own mind and the assumptions and habits he had formed in his own life. These methods are the basis and foundation of Buddhism in all its forms today. And it is because of this line of inquiry that Buddhism has never really been a sanctioning dogma for mass violence.

As a result of his stance about the absolute, people often make the erroneous conclusion that the Buddha did not believe in God. This is a misperception. Rather, what he was driving at was: As we cannot agree on who or what God is, let's not talk or argue or kill each other over or in the name of God. Instead, to really begin a spiritual journey to know God or anything absolute about "life, the universe, and everything," let's start with the territory between our ears and in our hearts; our own minds. Let us examine and transform the habitual tendencies, patterns, and all the stories we tell ourselves about who we are, who others are, what the world is about, etc. Let's try to awaken beyond the phantasm of our own creation. To see creation, to see God, to know what is and our place in it, we need to WAKE UP.

Waking up is about de-constructing fantasy.

Waking up is not about arriving somewhere else.

It's about being where you are fully.

I contend that the spiritual journey both within and without the context of religion arises from a desire or itch to do just this. We want to be happy. We become aware over time of some sense of alienation that we desire to overcome. As we mature, we see more and more clearly that the problems we face are the problems we have created. Thus all the esoteric aspects of the world religions that focus on these existential issues and dilemmas have their own path or methodology for tackling the mental and emotional confusion we encounter as we try to wake up. In these matters there is a commonality and the brother/sisterhood often felt amongst practitioners on this level is genuine, if not exhilarating. In these days I think that the methods taught and codified by the Buddha are universally respected and often applied in conjunction with the practices of other faiths not because only the Buddha was aware of them, but because few cultures have allowed the esoteric aspects of their religious systems to be available, except to a few. Thus in these days, when looking for methods to negotiate the road map and the terrain that all of us find ourselves in, the traditions of the Buddha seem most intact and available.

But, please be clear. All that said, I do not want anyone to think that the aspirants who call themselves Buddhist are immune from the follies and foibles of what happens when we as humans reify and deify our realities. Like all human endeavors, whilst there has never been a war waged on this planet in the name of Buddhism, this does not mean to say that ego and small minds have not similarly used Buddhist doctrine for less than holy ambitions. To this day, there are groups seeking sectarian superiority under the banner of this or that saint, someone claiming enlightened credentials, or a purer doctrine who market themselves to those attracted to and thirsty for absolutist security. In my discussion with a now deceased Korean Zen Master regarding some of these modern day groups and movements, he made a very succinct comment: "Bad idea."

To be totally transparent in my own relationship to my elected spiritual path – Tibetan Buddhism - this tradition has struggled with freeing itself from the feudal culture in which it was first fostered. In the post-diaspora crisis of the Chinese invasion, exiled Tibet Buddhism is still connected to and often sponsored by clans and families. Thus I have heard of murders, assassinations, land grabs, vendettas, and threat of hellish afterlife if not complied with all done in the name of this or that doctrine of the Buddha pepper what some wish to view as a pristine spiritual path. And sadly, these events implicate even some of the most revered. I shall never forget speaking with a very high teacher who explained how clan and family politics trump spiritual awareness, especially in a time when the culture strives to survive in exile. I do not doubt that there are unsavory deeds that need to be done which can only be understood from a more transcendent point of view. However, too often such actions have been covered by a cloak of inscrutability that neophytes are often expected to accept blindly in order to establish their faith in the path and unquestioning devotion to teachers, priests and the like. This is not just a Tibetan

Buddhist problem. Such dynamics plague any if not all institutions that seek to define the meanings by which we live. Indeed, in my long affiliation with the Tibetan Buddhist communities in the US and Europe, I too have had to endure and extricate myself from pecking order battles, sectarian pissing contests, and political wrangling. And I openly acknowledge that the disappointment of discovering and being embroiled in the all too human dramas within it have been an integral part in my awareness and resolve that one needs to be willing to separate the wheat from the chaff in all circumstances, including ones own tradition.

At an Ayurvedic conference held in Albuquerque, New Mexico, in a conversation with a friend about our spiritual journeys, he made an astute observation. At some point, each of us needs to "jump ship," or from my own experience, have a wise teacher burn our boat. The value of religion is that it holds together the practices, philosophies, and its practitioners as supports underneath our fledgling spiritual wings. And it does so, generation after generation. But, unless we jump ship or have our boats burned so that we can complete the journey, make it real in our own lives, if we stay around and get habituated to religious life rather than engage and work with spiritual practice, we shall find ourselves more and more immersed in politics, economics, and marketing. And, those who actualize the practice, those who come to really awaken from whichever path that they have been on will, sooner or later, become useless, a burden, or a danger to political, economic, and marketing efforts. That is why the greatest teachers and saints over the course of history have been viewed as outcasts, outlaws, heretics, apostates who have suffered whatever fate each tradition claims as just punishment for those who dare to live the laws from within rather than be dictated to from without. And the protected circle, the ones who ascribe to and live by the letter of the law reified and deified over time find that the faith they submit to eventually becomes a prison in which every possible human foible and vice will eventually makes itself known. For years I have said that there is nothing more political than a religious organization. Similarly, a religion that vehemently insists upon specifically dictated (from above) moral codes and mandated religious behaviors will find those who speak the loudest about them behind some of the most perverse of behavior. This is in keeping with the wisdom of modern-day Japanese Macrobiotic philosopher, Georges Ohsawa, who said, "What has a front, has a back. The bigger the front, the bigger the back."

What is unique about this time is not that sexual intrigue, political ambition, money laundering and the like still plague religious and spiritual circles. But, in a world where it is extremely rare – if ever it was even possible - to have a hermetically sealed reality free from outside influence or interference based on all the factors I have outlined in this book thus far, absolutist claims and the cloaks of secrecy that would have historically concealed less-than-holy ambitions are more known, challenged, and if nothing else, given much less legitimacy as would have been enjoyed in the past.

To summarize up to this point: The "chosen people" concept of any faith becomes highly suspect in a world where agreed upon absolutes which were at one time easier to enforce, have either become or hang on by a thread from being relativized. Secondly, such notions are not only implicitly unsubstantiated in a world of others who believe the same about themselves, they are downright dangerous and a threat to the overall well-being of a pluralistic society. Finally, the "it's all good" type of progressive talk that tries to shellac over everything as being the same from some hypothetically higher perspective, that we all have eyes on the same prize if we could only agree to live in a "kumbaya" kind of existence is not particularly helpful in overcoming such views. Beyond an agreement that each of us as humans have similar wants and needs, it is sloppy thinking that may be nice in ecumenical circles to keep the peace, but can also create naïve, wooly-minded numbed-ness when it comes to discerning and knowing how to handle the aspirations and ambitions of radical or extreme fundamentalist sects or cults of any or all faiths that show contempt for the common good and stand and have possibly historically demonstrated that a willingness to threaten the thriving and surviving of "others," if not all people and species on the planet in the name of their holy whatever. Furthermore, it overlooks the fact that there are many layers to spiritual life. Some may seek solace and assistance in enduring the vicissitudes of their personal fate or within a collective experience of persecution. Others may pray to uplift or empower their lives for more personal reward, satisfaction, or bliss. Others may seek a feeling of connection with some transcendent reality. Others feeling a connection with all that is around them may focus altruistically on the welfare of others. In all of the expressions of spiritual life, there are levels of intention. But, the bottom line of all is to feel a greater sense of happiness in life.

That there are distinctions in the levels of the spiritual and/or invisible worlds that we as humans relate to may seem inconsequential to many in a post-industrial world, who have become cynical about religion in general and consequently disregard or ignore feelings beckoning them towards their spiritual birthright. Thus whilst the United States remains a nation where a significant percentage of the population still goes to church or synagogue (estimated 30-40%), Europe, more intimately familiar with the trappings and pitfalls of organized religion is – by-and-large – secular (approximately 4% going to churches, etc.), if not highly suspicious of even esoteric or spiritual rhetoric. As a personal experience of this example, during a training of our company to teach Ayurvedic bodywork techniques to a major spa in France, my wife and I were informed that one of our treatments, a chakra stone treatment, could not use the term "chakra" because that was considered occult. We could also not use the word "karma" in our foot treatment, "PediKarma."

In spite of such cultural wariness and cynicism, owing to our innate loving nature and a quality of education that encourages critical thinking, morality based on humanistic principles, a "god-less" Europe leads the world in quality universal healthcare, environmental initiatives to slow down the ravages of global warming, and charitable contributions to aid efforts in disasters around the world. In essence, in contrast to how far behind the United States lags when it comes to affordable and preventive-based healthcare and serious environmental action, it would seem that Europe has generally chosen to steer by a moral compass guided by an internal reference point that makes their societies more aware of personal and collective

103

responsibility. Of course this is not universally true. And it would seem that zealots and xenophobes are on the rise in Europe at this time. The distinction and point being made here, however, is critical.

I may be wary of God as an external reference point – a Big Daddy in the sky to obey or a Big mamma upon whose breast I am suppose to suckle for my sustenance – but, I am not an atheist. Not even an agnostic. Furthermore, I believe that having some faith or notion in a transcendent, spiritual, or invisible world or worlds beyond ourselves and the three dimensional world our senses are generally limited to perceiving, matters. Thus I cannot be a Marxist or Maoist in overtly condemning religion as poison – unless it runs ramshackle over the beauty of our spiritual being-ness, leaves us quaking in fear and subservience, and subverts or minimizes our sense of personal responsibility over our lives. If any faith does such, I have no problem in saying that such religions are pathetic.

While it is true that science has reached into space and down into the center of the atom to eliminate or sufficiently explain things which were originally attributed to gods, demons, spells, curses, and the like, it would be arrogant to assume that if we keep expanding the doors of inquiry that we shall eventually know it all. The fact is that we may come to understand the mechanisms behind most things, but we cannot even to this day answer <u>why</u> these mechanisms and the things they are attributed to exist in the first place. In spite of the vastness of his knowledge of the operations of the universe, Albert Einstein proclaimed that it had given him a greater belief in a God and something beyond himself.

But even if we are not an Einstein, the simple fact is that where our knowledge fails us – mostly in the big events of life (i.e. birth, death, and the inevitable unexpected twists and turns of life that few if any of us are immune to) – our cleverness brings us little joy or confidence. On the edge of the unknown, if we have no sense of wonder, no sense of a world greater than what our intellect and ego will allow, then we meet these events unprepared to cope, endure, and otherwise traverse with peace or grace. For it is certain that life's trials, tribulations, and the bigger transitional events that inevitably challenge or bodies and minds will carry or push us into waters uncharted.

In my life, I have been fortunate to be present with the birth of all of my children as well as those of friends. If drugs, orgasm, or a numinous experience have not shown a woman the vastness of a world far greater, transition in the birthing process, if done in as natural way as it is possible for her to deal with, is a gateway. In this way, I am humbled and feel that women have a great advantage over men when it comes to these matters – which is probably why few men were ever burned as witches.

On the other side of the spectrum, as a hospice social worker, I have been with people who meet the light seen at death with grace and others who are terrorized by it. I have also seen people with very clear, but rigid beliefs they have been inculcated with through their faiths have them torn asunder and feel abandoned by God or discover that what they believe was not what seemed to be waiting for them.

105

In regard to these latter situations, it tells me that to not train to turn to internal, developed skills of insight and awareness during life creates an over-reliance of images and concepts that have never really, truly touched our hearts or been tested. Then again, I have seen people who are open minded but have never professed a faith of any sort who, standing on the edge of death, stare at wonderment as they come to see and realize that what they are about to be released into is far greater than what they may have been taught and feel, as a result, great peace and joy.

The world is more multi-dimensional than most of us can get our heads around, let alone navigate. To shrink away from a transcendent and invisible world and only believe in our man-made, ego driven laws and conventions is to cut ourselves off from the vastness of which we are a part and minimize and discredit our continuous, ongoing connection and communication with a world that offers us limitless possibilities – if we only understand how to better interact with it.

This is what I would like to address next.

Chapter Four

Working Model of Oneness

You've read my story and have heard about all the many traditions and perspectives I have encountered and been influenced by along the way. You also probably have some sense of my orientation when it comes to spirituality and religion. The life I was brought into, the people and circumstances, and the intellectual and philosophical musings I have shared have all created in me an integral model of the transcendent or spiritual dimensions of life of which it should be clear at this point I do not see as in any way separate from the mundane reality most of our minds muse around in.

It would be totally presumptuous and arrogant for me to say that this is how it is. Rather, I would say that I have "faith" that this is how it is. I say "faith" rather than believe because the verb "believe" implies a set of "beliefs" which form the basis for dogma – that which unfortunately arises when the snapshot of perception and conception is reified, deified and carried forward in time, too often not truly tested. All dogmas are highly suspect and eventually self-destruct as does the world of the proponents, champions, and enforcers if they cannot come to a more flexible, agreeable, and humorous relationship with impermanence.

My faith is, therefore, based on working assumptions. I say "working" because I am still looking, opening, surrendering in the wake of all the stories I have told myself about myself, others, and the world I live in. This is the impermanent and ever expanding world my heart and brain is cascading through. And considering that the influences in my culture and circumstances are not that dissimilar from the pluralistic relativized world of thoughts, ideas, and - to a greater or lesser extent - experiences as outlined earlier, perhaps my process and the conclusions I am working with based on that process will be useful for you. If nothing else, I hope it sparks some curiosity.

But, before I start, I would like to share a story that illustrates the inclusivity of thought and process I think is vital for sane, responsible, sustainable and beneficial personal spiritual development and the seeding of our collective future.

In the mid-eighties, while I was working as a body worker, biofeedback therapist and nutritional counselor at a holistic health center in Lexington, Kentucky, brothers from the Gethsemane Trappist Monastery in Trappist, Kentucky invited me to come to their hermitage to help them create a better menu for their aging brothers. I was honored to do so as this was the monastery of the late, great Thomas Merton.

In the two days that I was there, in my off time I took advantage of the solitary retreat that they housed me in for guests. There I did my Tibetan Buddhist meditations. But, I also decided to join the brothers in some of their prayer life. Thus for two days, at 3:00am, I attended vespers. I did not take communion, not because I did not want to, but because the abbot, knowing that I was not Catholic, did not think it appropriate. As the Catholic notion of communion is in the same spirit of the feasts or ganachakra practices of Tantric Buddhism, it would have been

– in my own eyes - fine for me to accept that the wafer and wine was the body and blood of Christ and partake. But, the abbot was the one holding the goblet.

During the working part of the day I was in the kitchen with cooks and assistants to the kitchen. We did spend some of our time developing a healthier menu. But, an equal amount of time was spent talking about the role of meditation and yoga in these brothers' lives.

Zen Buddhist meditation and hatha yoga being practiced by the Catholic Trappist monks in Thomas Merton's monastery in the predominantly fundamentalist Christian hills of Kentucky. Their reasoning? Anything that they could do to quiet their minds and bodies and experience God and deepen their faith in Jesus Christ was fine by them. These devoted souls had traveled all over the country to attend yoga and Zen retreats. There was no contradiction, no conflict in their minds about this, just synthesis, integration, and transformation. Thomas Merton would have been proud of these men.

In the spirit of these wonderful brothers, I offer these observations and reflections. I shall do this by addressing various spiritually related topics in this and the following chapter.

God

Let's start with God.

But, first of all I have to admit that up until recently I had a difficult time even mentioning the word God. For one thing, it is such a loaded term, meaning different things to different people. And as a Buddhist in my adult years, I have grown accustomed to not using the term in relation to spiritual growth and development. This has to do with the Buddhist sense of personal responsibility; of being the masters of our own ship. And as I have stated earlier, if there is an external reference point that we abdicate to over the course and actions of our lives, it is easy to stray off into places where stiff ideas and justifications become sanctified. All this said, Buddhist thought may not reference the God of creation as conveyed in the book of Genesis, but it does not decry or deny the existence of such. Thus, with my Jewish roots still playing in the background of my being, I see no other term that best describes what I wish to describe here other than the word, God.

I believe that God *is* everything and God is everywhere. There is no separation between God and us. In this respect, I guess I am a gnostic, although I feel that the term used by Gnostics – light – is limiting. Nevertheless, it works well enough. Thus in the great light of God, we are shards, fragments, waves, or particles of that very same stuff. The separation we feel, the isolation that leads to desperation, that creates big and small, strong and weak egos, that makes us do horrible as well as exquisite things to each other and all that is around us that is God as well – is illusory. This illusion is based on misperception. In the true rather than the condemning definition that reinforces that sense of separation, we are sinners. To sin is to be off the mark. We haven't got it right, that's all. Buddhists say that this misperception is the result of Three Poisons; ignorance, attachment, and aggression; that is, we don't know what is going on, we get attached to some small ego-based view of what we think is going on, and we are willing to fight to defend, promote, or annihilate others whose opinion differs from ours.

Misperception is a function of maturity. Maturity comes about as we awaken more and more to the light within us. Our own process moving from birth to death will – of its own accord – reveal this light through the gift of impermanence. It will also occur through us bumping into and learning how to relate to that which we initially see as separate from us. Thus, inner movement and outer interaction sets up endless perpetual opportunities. But none of these opportunities come to fruition as awakening moments until, through trials, tribulations, and teachings along the way we learn to come to a stillness within.

This stillness we <u>all</u> know to be who we are, in spite of our habitual mind trying to convince us otherwise. It is the light within that is none other than and not separate from God. Thus when awakening occurs and the evolutionary step – which by the way is not sequential or fixed as one set progression – dissolves the illusory duality that most beings not yet awakened live in, the shift that has occurred is a place from which one may periodically flounder or stray, but will eventually become stabilized from the work that now becomes the only reasonable thing to do. From the place of duality such a view and living looks foreign, divergent, heretical, which is why – not surprisingly - those who wake up are so often banished, martyred, crucified, sent to outcast land.

Awakening to the inseparability between ourself and God, we understand that there is no sacred versus profane; that the sacred arises from alignment and the profane a diversion that comes about through a lack of maturity. There is no absolute or unconditional reality that does not reveal itself but through relative circumstances calling us to a higher intention; calling us back to God. What this means is that we are ALL a part of God. While we might not always do what is seemingly right or best, this does not stop us from being or negate the fact that we are God. Thus, putting ourselves or another down, treating others as being better or lesser than us, denigrating or taking advantage of circumstance, resources, and so forth is to not see the divinity in all.

Furthermore, even the space-time continuum of an expanding universe that I have described in a previous chapter is nothing more than the way in which our sense fields, organs and the sensing technology we have thus far created (which is really nothing more than extensions of the constructs of our senses as we know them), are instruments through which we gather information that reveals a life far greater than our perceptions or beliefs have thus far identified with. That is, other than to us, is a universe expanding? Are stars flying apart and worlds being created? Is there a divine symmetry and mathematical precision in everything? Or, do these constructs, like fingers pointing at the moon merely serve as aids to direct us homeward; that that which we construe as beauty and to marvel at it is one of the joys in the process of discovering and living in the truth of inseparability. But, we must be aware that it is still just a process. We must never settle on the constructs of our perceptions and conceptions as the end of the road, the omega destination where we park and hang out. If we ever think that we have "gotten" there, we are at just one more relative destination and we are still looking at the finger than the moon. Fortunately for us, bliss may be a personal experience of that awakening that comes from discovering or uncovering the light under the layer upon layer of delusion that has no beginning, whilst the feeling JOY offers a relational dimension. Connection is obvious, unequivocal, and feels good. These feelings, bliss, joy, and goodness give us a sense of lightness along the way. And whilst we may ascribe such feelings to mundane events and experiences along the way, if that to which we ascribe these experiences are not the real deal, these feelings will erode or implode as their opposites. We are in an endless, benevolent feedback loop constantly directing us home. We shall explore this further in the next chapter. Bu, for now, back to God.

Similar to Lao Tzu's notion of the Uncarved Block, my notion of God is that to use a pronoun of he, she, or it conjures sex or neuter-dom, attributes to appease our conceptual frameworks. To even say that God is creator and all that is created conjures a notion of what may be uncreated – a dualism that is unsubstantiated, but problematic nevertheless.

For me there is no distinction between the Uncarved Block, the Buddhist notion of Suchness, and the Judeo-Christian notion of a Supreme Being – if you take the notion of "being" as not being a thing or entity, but rather a state. And while all the world's religions may debate over various attributes of who and what God is, one quality stands out as universal and that is LIGHT. This light is not only a matter of what is seen (i.e. the light of God as when dying and wanting to go to God we encourage our loved ones to go to the light) but also of weight – as in lightness of being. At the same time, this light does not imply a dualistic opposite, ie. darkness or heaviness, the polarities arising from a dualistic perspective. Rather what is not light is – in my mind – a nascent, less complete or mature manifestation of light. Even entropic thinking that may revel in dualism is, again, just making its own sweet way to light. Thus, as an extrapolation of this premise, as, a good Buddhist, I cannot accept that anything or anyone is entirely dark or evil. To hold onto the God versus Satan story as the game that is going and the one that has to be played forever pits us in an unending, losing battle. This does not mean that what is woefully astray and divergent from light, that which causes pain and suffering, should not be confronted. But to do so in the belief that one is eradicating such forces now or forever is to lose sight of the deeper purpose in making the effort. It is said that in a mind state of Suchness, the Samurai notes that before he lies down to sleep, there is blood on the edge of his sword. Whatever has been done has only served light. In the end, it is erroneous duality itself that needs to be eradicated.

When I was at university in Cleveland and considering becoming a rabbi and join my ancestral lineage's calling, I was either blessed or cursed with a crusty curmudgeon as an Old Testament professor. His analysis of this, one of Western civilization's most revered books, was far from dry, but virtually barren of any particular positive or negative emotion or thought process to favor or disfavor what he had meticulously investigated a good part of his life. He did not care what you did or did not believe. He just wanted you to understand this holy of holies as an inspired piece of literature within the social, historical, and political context of the time in which it was scribed. His point was for us to understand as best as possible what was true and factual so that each student in the classroom could then look at what they assumed or believed and come to a more informed, grounded or substantiated basis for faith. And the life, roles, and actions of God as elaborated in the Bible were just facets which he had no hesitation in looking at with his old, unflinching academic astuteness.

If you were to walk down the street of any place where you can factor in the homogeneity of the population in the area and ask them about who or what God is, chances are there would be some overlaps, but there would also be a lot of personal interpretation so that the picture and attributes of God may make one person's notion of God indistinguishable to another person's view. Similarly, what my university professor revealed was inconsistency in the portrayal of God. But not only that, it lead one to wonder if the creator God of Genesis is the same god referred to in Exodus when Moses is handed down the Ten Commandments or earlier in the Bible where Abraham's faith is tested in his willingness to sacrifice his son, Isaac.

A god testing your loyalty. A god saying that he is a jealous god. And, you better not bad-mouth him. I'm not too sure that I want to have anything to do with this character. Then again, in the culture of the time, was this just a useful allegory to make a point rather than to point to God?

In the second Commandment, along with him being jealous, this god talks about not having any other god before him. While so many who advocate monotheism and say there is only one god, god here is implying that there are others – none as great as he, of course – but out there, in the heavens, on the land, under the seas.

Before elaborating on this too much, I would like to address the issue of one god and many gods. For, I think that as this commandment has been misinterpreted, it has convinced monotheistic believers that their god is the only god going. This god has all of the positive attributes that we can think of for an omniscient, omnipresent, and omnipotent. With such a myopic awareness, one can come to the erroneous conclusion that other gods, buddhas, elementals or anything else that may have influence over the world we live in are just fictitious. They don't exist, but in the mind of heathens, psychotics, and/or simpletons. Or, they are the many faces of Satan.

Years ago I was teaching a class on the Tibetan Buddhist practice on the Buddha known as the Medicine Buddha. This Buddha apparently achieved his awaken state way before the creation of our known universe. And it is said that he lives in Sudarshan, an enlightened realm in distant space.

One of the students of the class asked me, "Is this for real? Does the Medicine Buddha really exist?"

My answer: "He exists just as much as we do."

In "The Bigger Story," I have shown that you are made mostly of space, that where you are is never in the same place, and that it is because of the Three Poisons of ignorance, attachment, and aggression that we get some very strange, funny, and sometimes even tragic ideas about who, what, and where we are, thus limiting our perception of all realms, visible as well as invisible, something we shall discuss at length in a forthcoming chapter.

All this said, if you really don't know who or what you are and what you are is more than you ever imagined, can you be so certain that other realms of existences based on different levels of perception and physicality do not exist? Are these buddhas, gods, elementals mere archetypes, metaphors, or are they actually real – just as real as us?

With all this in mind, let's get back to looking at God and gods...

The Tibetan Buddhist tradition draws a distinction between the enlightened, awakened realms beyond duality and the realms where duality and its resulting suffering abide. In this dualistic reality, there are a number of realms of understanding, governed by different states of mind, matured to whatever degree they have matured to. There are hell beings dominated by anger and fear, ghosts obsessively caught up in unfulfilled desires, animals that live in a hunted and be hunted world of reflexive habitual responses, human such as ourselves whose minds are dominated by passion and desire, titans or demi-gods who are jealous and want more, and gods whose good fortune makes them proud and aloof. Each of us knows these states of mind as we all go through every one of the emotions ascribed to each of these realms. However, imagine what it would be like if one of these emotions – other than the desire and passion you have as a human - was your dominant mode of operation and response. Laws of karma, which we shall describe in detail in the next chapter, delivers us into one of these realms based on our responses to what life hands us to cope with.

Here I only wish to comment on worldly gods and demi-gods in the most general of ways as they relate to the God that I am a part of. More about them will be discussed in a subsequent chapter.

If you have sown what you have reaped and end up in a god realm in the world of duality, you are in a place where beings have accumulated enough good fortune to have perfect, "almost" immortal bodies as a result of having performed many good deeds, but mostly to make themselves look good or important in front of others. They like to be prayed to and praying to them can have benefits as they do have powers of control over phenomenon. But overall, they stand a bit aloof, out of the fray, not wanting to get their hands dirty, just enjoying their beautiful, perfect bodies and their bliss-filled minds in paradises human literature fantasizes, dreams, and drools over.

Then, there are the demi-gods. The demi-gods wish they were gods. Thus, they are jealous, competitive. They periodically war with the gods because they want what is not theirs. Demi-gods are insecure and want to be loved and venerated. A god that tests you to see if you are willing to kill for him, who is jealous, and possibly fickle, first choosing you as a chosen people, then dumping you to create a second covenant because the new people follow his only begotten son, and then supposedly dump these new people because these 2 covenants are not the real deal, but the one he is choosing to have with you is because you have the true faith seems pretty insecure to me. This does not sound like a great, omniscient, omnipresent, omnipotent being.

So much bickering and bloodshed between and wrought by the sons of Abraham in the name of or for the glory of God: the lineage I am descended from. With all the versions and interpretations at various points in the Bible as to the attributes of god, what if most of us most of the time have it wrong? If fear and wrath is how this god rules and/or the one that many of the chosen decide to back, this is not the God of creation that I am willing to open my heart up to.

Do I risk hellfire and damnation for saying this? Perhaps. I do not have the strength or abilities of a god or demi-god. So, I could be really screwed. Then again, for those who believe in such a god, my words are an abomination, a heresy – in which case my biggest concern may not be divine retribution, but the ordinary human garden-variety type.

Bearing this in mind, that the qualities, actions, and allegiances to this or that image of god or gods comes out of the minds of humans who may just be divinely inspired, but more often than not are not, perhaps none of this can be laid on God or any gods' door for that matter. What if all this is early neuro-linguistic programing (NLP)? What if it is just really good marketing? What if all the claims and descriptions about who God is and is not, who he likes and who he claims is going to heaven and who to hell is just human contrivance subject to the winds of change and embellished over the years by those who hold the Bible, the Koran, the Bhagavad

Gita, or any other holy book for that matter up as a testament to their power and authority to justify getting what they or a group or a nation want on this planet?

My conclusion in my ponderings is that there is – in Masonic terms – the Grand Supreme Architect or Creator that we are all a part of. In our evolution as individuals, we go through stages of individual and collective insecurities that lead us to create time-borne and dependent absolutes, reified and deified concepts and myths. Inevitably, in our ever-changing impermanent world these myths and concepts outlive their usefulness and are proven wrong or – at the least – no longer effective. Taking what was only metaphor to start with as literal and trying to enforce what is a world view that is all but a shadow of the times we are in, so much misery is engendered and damage done to the human psyche and family, which, considering that wise words and counsel are far less heeded than suffering and disaster, may not actually be as big a problem as progressive minds may think. That is, perhaps a good slap up the side of the head is the best strategy to wake us out of our smugness and complacency.

Furthermore, that there are gradations of other beings – gods, demi-gods, and others who likewise inhabit this ALL that we are a part of and – just like us – and are working out for themselves their place through the process of awakening.

That said, when someone says that they worship God and question or challenge you about the same, a fair and reasonable question to ask or consider is what god are they referring to? This may take people aback because the simple truth is that – like the wise men touching part of an elephant while blind-folded – what is meant by and what attributes are given to god vary even amongst those who pay their dues or tithe to the same church, temple, or mosque.

That I am a part of and never separate from God is a statement that I can feel great joy in, but do not say glibly. In fact, it is a statement that I use cautiously because the process to become free from the constraints of convention and reified thinking and concepts can come from motivations that lead to a lightening of fixation on a personal ego or the opposite; ie. an even more entrenched ego. Buddhist teachers warn of mistaking Rudra-hood (Rudra being someone who attained complete, self-centered, supreme ego-hood) for Buddhahood. In this respect and in the same light, a good friend and respected psychiatrist with many years of wisdom says that many of the most disturbed mentally ill criminals he has worked with over the years believe that they are Jesus Christ or God. And consider the movie "Natural Born Killers" where extricating themselves from the constraints of bad religion and abusive family and horrific circumstances, a man and a woman support each other in acts of revenge where they feel freer and erroneously conclude that further acts like this will make them even freer still.

Thus, for me the most important safeguard from going off the deep end where individual ego is fed rather than deconstructed into a greater openness and qualities exemplifying wisdom and compassion is the ongoing practice of some form of contemplative and meditation. Consider the monks of Gethsemane.

Soon after Hurricane Katrina wiped out so much of New Orleans, I can remember hearing TV evangelists claiming that New Orleans had been destroyed because of our iniquities; that we allowed abortion, accepted gays in the military, and so on. A few weeks later, the Jehovah's Witnesses who came to my door asked me if I thought God was responsible for what happened in New Orleans.

I told them that in the grand scheme of things, God has got a lot to do and there are all sorts of ways that He needs to take care of the planet. Large and small weather and geo-physical events such as hurricanes, tornadoes, and earthquakes to keep things in balance, et cetera. There have always been such events. The stars and planets are zipping through space. This is just how a planet rocks and rolls. That said, that humans decide to build a city close to an ocean below sea level shows a lack of understanding and may even be rather hubristic: that as stewards appointed by God over the planet, that we can get away with such things. But more than that, if we then expect administrators to year after year be scrupulous and honest in tending to the levees that protect its citizens, we are also living in a fantasy realm.

I watch reports of the devastation of tornadoes in America's Midwest. There are miracle stories of those saved who believe their safety was an act of God whilst others raise their fists to the sky and ask why God has forsaken them. And, no one steps back to take into consideration the fact that based on any number of factors, tornadoes are a part of this terrain and that construction practices in the area should take this into consideration. And, if you don't want tornadoes at all, move somewhere else.

I think of Kobe, Japan – destroyed about every 100 years from earthquakes only to be rebuilt by those who do not want to live anywhere else. And, there are people who live at the base of volcanoes.

Then there is me, living on the San Andreas fault line nine miles from a nuclear power station...

So, standing on two precipices of doom, I do not blame God for any of this. To pray to God to stop tornadoes, hurricanes, and earthquakes or to stop them just for me, my friends and/or fellow followers is just a waste of prayer and rather self-centered. In the long run, such unrealistic wishes only lead to disappointment and disempowerment. And when a sense of spiritual connection is destroyed, it is much harder for us to accept ourselves as spiritual beings, just having a human experience.

Living in a godless existence, where you do not have to believe that there is a divine eye or some god shaking his head looking over your shoulder may seem a relief for a time. But, when the bigger questions arise over the larger events of our short time on this planet – birth, life-challenging illnesses, and death – to not have a sense of connection to something greater than our own body and emotions usually proves itself to be insufficient to the task of finding meaning in it all.

Connection, authorship, and responsibility; all of these are big issues for which we want and don't want easy answers.

An old Tibetan adage says it is easier to put on shoes than to cover the world in leather. That is, you cannot prepare for every eventuality, especially if you believe that you are separate from your world, and that someone needs to always be there to protect you from every one of life's vicissitudes. More than likely, were this really the case, we would fall asleep at the wheel of our own lives. We would become smug, indifferent, and judgmental – so long as everything was going our way. We may be able to get away with this kind of self-righteous stupor periodically, but as George Harrison put it, "All Things Must Pass." In the long run, preparing our hearts and minds to more nobly and humanely engage such events, many of which we shall ALL have to face, seems the most logical way to go.

PRE-DESTINATION or FREE WILL?

For too long the theological debate over whether our lives are merely pre-destined or that it is all in our hands and we can chose however we want it to be – hence have total free will – has seemingly "perplexed" philosophers and theologians over the centuries. As we have never inquired or asked any of these esteemed individuals their biases and why, I don't that we are really earnest to use our bright minds and hearts to get to the bottom of the big "it all." In my mind, I see this pondering and polemic as a rather bogus issue. How I see it is that when we are feeling puny or want to rationalize why we hold others in a station below ourselves (i.e. slaves, the caste system, etc.), then pre-destination seems to be the philosophical stance that wins the day. And, when we are on top of things and life is going just the way we want it to and/or we see someone we are in competition with lose in whatever way we think they should, then free will is our best buddy. Thus, the argument of these two philosophical stances is much less about a big picture, and more to do with our own current version and how we feel about our lives in general.

In this very expanding, ever changing, very impermanent world of which we are a part and that being none other than a part - a shard - of the God to which I ascribe, my gradual awakening - the maturation of my shard of light in the grand light of it all - takes into account every direct step and diversion I take along my life path. I do not believe that this has to do with pre-destination, a planned out clear and unerring plan. Rather, due to circumstances and my habitual patterns and reactions to those circumstances, there are greater and lesser likely mathematical probabilities that bring me closer or further to the fruition of complete awakening. Then again, I cannot be too sure if this is not just an evolutionary process hidden from my perceptions and conceptions and that the path is like a labyrinth where the seeming close is actually far and the seeming far is actually close to the center, i.e. symbolic of awakening. Similarly I ponder the notion of free will and see it, too, as a notion circumscribed by probabilities. Nature behaves in given ways and although there are seeming anomalies, most of all of what is possible will play itself out in a field proscribed by the limitations of the Grand Design of which I know so little, yet know that I am a part of.

What seems most evident to me in these considerations is that I am a co-creator and co-participant in whom the illusion of separation from such brings suffering whilst the acceptance of inclusion brings joy and a sense of limitless possibility. Personally, if what and how I think is circumscribed, even directed by a Supreme

Being, the only thing that is really being hurt by such thinking is my limited ego that may have in its habitual programming an inflated sense of who and what I am in the scheme of things. But, if I then throw all caution to the wind and act in a bohemian way believing that I have no control or part in what I am doing, then I lose sight of the light that is within me that that is the best possible indicator or feedback mechanism of whether the course of my life is moving towards or away from awakening.

In the deliberations of such matters and the choices we make along the way, what moves us one way or the other? What makes us attracted to light or dark, positive or questionable influences? Why do we have the preferences that we do? Why is our life the way it is? And lastly, who's in charge here?

If we are not separate from God, then the "my will" versus "thy will" conundrum is a mute point. It all then comes down to what's happening. As vague as this may sound, the sense behind such becomes clearer as we look into what in the east is known as KARMA and the place and role of morality. This is what we shall discuss next.

Chapter Five

What You're Sowing and Where You're Going

(Karma, Reincarnation, and Our Inner Moral Compass)

KARMA is one of those misunderstood and misused words. As I mentioned earlier, when teaching in France, we could not call one of our Ayurvedic treatments that we developed and teach by the name we commonly use; PediKarma. We were told that the term "karma" is considered occult, thus unacceptable in certain public quarters and definitely nothing that could be written on a spa treatment menu. Of course, this did not mean that the word "karma" was banned, but rather that certain clientele would never do a treatment by that name, some clientele may never come back, and some would never even darken the door to the spa for fear that the spa may be practicing witchcraft or making massage oils from boiled toads.

There are those, however, who bandy the word about and use "karma" as an excuse for passive acceptance or non-intervention – despite the fact that the word actually means *action*, plain and simple. I have been in situations where I have heard amongst folks who consider their selves to be informed and "in tune" or "connected" who would glibly say that the starvation experienced by some in Africa or elsewhere in the world is just their karma. On a very objective level, although this may be true, an understanding of the "karmic" connection to that situation escapes these people's reasoning and lacks humanity. My response to those who think in this way is that they have the karma of having apathy.

When the concept of karma comes up in conversations, some people roll their eyes, not wanting to listen to some New Age dribble. Then there are others who express outrage over this concept. How can karma be a factor when people find themselves in dire circumstances? Did children ask to be born in the refugee camps of Somalia? What about rape or incest? How can anyone say that a victim has some part in what horror he or she experiences at the hand of another? To suggest such as a possibility evokes moral outrage.

It is for all these reasons that we need to look at this word karma and get a better understanding of rebirth or reincarnation, and morality – in that order.

KARMA

As mentioned above, KARMA means *action* and the "laws" of karma are about skillfully acting and seeing what actions or *reactions* flow from what we do. In this regard, karma is no different from the biblical adage, "What you sow, so shall you reap." However, what is useful for us is that Buddhist mind science wisdom breaks karma down into intelligible parts so that we can understand the mechanisms at work in its making.

The Four Parts of Karma

There are four parts or steps in every action. And how we navigate through each and every step determines what comes back at us – feedback from our world. These four are...

1. Intention/Motivation

2. Planning

3. Action

4. Reflection; our own reaction (feelings and thoughts) about what we have done.

Bear in mind that that this mechanism is neither good nor bad. It just is. One thing leads to another. The issue is always how awake are we to the process to bring about something that is beneficial rather than harmful.

So let's start at the beginning with intention and/or motivation.

Something happens in our world to which we want or feel compelled to respond to. Or perhaps, what may seem out of the clear blue, we decide we should do or create something. In the long run and from a more detached perspective, these two are not that dissimilar. The major point is that there is an impetus within us to act.

What is that impetus? Looking at a full range of human emotions, are we angry and want to retaliate? Do we want to make peace or ignore the situation? Are we jealous and feel like we deserve what the other person has? Are we lustful and just want what we want because we want it? Are we prideful and just think that whatever is going on should go our way? On the positive end of the intention spectrum, are we excited and feeling creative? Do we want to extend compassion, kindness, exhibit patience, or desire to create peace and joy?

What is the state of our mind? And what intent does this state of mind create in us when we think of another or a situation? Do we want to help, harm, nurture, support, etc.?

Out of this state of mind we plan what we are going to do. This may be as short and un-thought out as a knee-jerk reflexive reaction or animalistic-instinctive response born out of a triggered survival (fight/flight) mechanism. On the other end of the spectrum, there could be much deliberation and planning into how you are going to act to perhaps initiate or respond from an external prompting; basically what you are going to DO next. So much goes into this step; emotions, knowledge, assumptions – the details you think you are in control of - and a varying degree of awareness as to what you do not have control over in what you plan to do. Thus there is a wide degree of what you think and how you plan that comes from a present awareness or habitual patterns that the circumstance is just triggering and beckoning us on in an almost auto-pilot fashion.

Then there is action, executing what you have planned. Whereas planning requires knowledge, action requires skill. Do we have the abilities it takes to execute a planned action successfully?

In planning and action we are attempting to fulfill our intentions to create the desired effect or outcome. The simple fact is, though, that few of us really have the time, the leisure, or presence of mind to thoroughly go through these steps with mindfulness with respect to so much of our lives. Other than in attempting to plan out specific events, most of the time our actions are reactions or partially thought out responses. That is, depending on what the circumstances are that we are dealing with, most of the time our responses or actions are actually rather random stemming from historical data and our habitual responses to that data – in which case, what comes back at us, the feedback we get from the world is often quite predictable – if we are honest with ourselves. This is summed up in an adage I was taught years ago...

"If you always do what you've always done, you'll always get what you've always gotten."

Unless we have been infused with or trained in a mindfulness tradition or culture, more often than not we are not fully present to situations that we find ourselves in. It would be fantastic and a sign of our awakened potential if our conscious choices were *really* conscious rather than being under the influence of habitual processes and subconscious emotional patterns. But, this is where most of us are. Even in approaching something that is new, we try to fix what is new into some familiar scheme, then reference the new situation with our prior responses. This has evolutionary benefits. We don't have to re-invent the wheel over and over again. But, it also stifles our ability to handle novelty or new situations. Even if we intend a different outcome, the fact that our planning and action comes out of habitual responses and emotional reactions, outcomes we get may be more familiar to us, but more than likely not the outcome we wanted or intended.

Thus, the final step in the process of karma comes from own response to that which we have done. Are we satisfied, pleased, frustrated, angry, content, confused, disappointed, etc. with the result or affect of what we have done? Has our action done what we intended it to do? If it did, does it feel complete or does it feel like it has lead to other things to think about? Did what you do unleash other unintended consequences, perhaps beneficial, perhaps harmful?

Looking a bit more closely...

We can see that in the range of intentions and motivations, we can come from a place within ourselves that can be selfish or altruistic, nefarious or magnanimous, mal-intended or well intended, and a variety of mixtures in between. Our planning steered by those motivations demands of us a knowledge base sufficient to know what we want to do and have a knowledge of all factors around that planned event or action. We act and then have a sense within ourselves of that act's effectiveness which in turns leads us to have an emotional reaction.

The result of this four-fold process, what could be called a karmic deed creates karmic seeds. That is, as a result of what we have done and how we feel about it, the "big wheel keeps on turnin'" and the seed planted by our actions is carried along to a point in the future that is most suited and accepting of it blossoming.

Although there are some amazing Buddhist texts that expound on karma and what deeds lead to what seeds or results, I would rather write here in generalities. I would like to say that I do not believe that any action is 100 percent good or 100 percent evil. In a relative world I think most if not all actions fall within a gradation of actions or karmic deeds that are harmful to those that are beneficial, that lead to their appropriate consequences. And while I see the need for judges, juries, and the consequence of incarceration, I think that regardless of whether we get caught or not for something heinous, the consequence will bear itself out in our lives irrespective of whether or not our human eye and legal systems pay attention or look the other way. As the Buddha once said, "Karma is infallible." The Bible concurs.

The most harmful karmic deeds are where – for example – you hate someone and want to see them dead, you plot to kill them, you have the skill and opportunity and take the opportunity to do the deed, and finally that you are thoroughly pleased that you wasted someone.

The most beneficial karmic deed would be where out of love and compassion you want to help someone, you plan a way to help them out, you have the skill and opportunity and take the opportunity to do your deed, and then rejoice in seeing them benefit.

So here we have what would be considered a black karmic deed and a white karmic deed. These deeds are events that flow from and flow into events that led us to the point of our action and flow from the deed we have done. Based on this logic, it stands to reason that where we end up next based on these two deeds would be very different – although perhaps not that apparent right afterwards. Perhaps the killer in the black deed scenario feels so happy that he books a flight to the Bahamas, where he meets a cute and available supermodel and has an enjoyable fling in the lap of luxury. Perhaps the person who did something good is in a peaceful and happy state and while riding his bike, gets hit by a drunk driver and dies.

Bringing up such examples will often in theological circles or in a thoughtful conversation at a wine bar or café lead to a discussion that starts with "Why do good things happen to bad people and bad things happen to good people?" Sadly, such a question does not step back to look at a bigger picture. For one thing, it looks at events in our lives sequentially and two dimensionally. A may lead to B. But the B we are linking to A may be the wrong A. In the case of our hit man, maybe he did a good deed for his landlady and her dog and that is why he is having fun in the Bahamas. And the B that leads from his hit (A) may be on its way, but not yet. Maybe the untimely death of our good fellow is connected to another event where – at some point – he accidently did harm to someone unwittingly.

But, let us focus on the black deed and the white deed as I originally described. If we take our four-point analysis of karma, what if any one of the points described in our examples changes?

Let's say that you hate someone, plan his or her demise, do the deed, but then realize that it hasn't made you happier or that you see the pain and anguish in the dead person's wife, mother, or father. You feel terrible. You want to repent. You decide to change your life. You confess and go to jail or confess in a confessional and turn your life over to Christ and do acts of charity. Or, maybe you are a soldier who actually doesn't hate the person. It's just your job to do this. So, you plan the deed, do it, and are satisfied, but perhaps not happy that you fulfilled your assignment. In both these scenarios, the killing took place, but your intention or motivation and/or your response to having done the deed are different.

Taking the white deed. You love someone, plan to help them, do the deed, but you are really disappointed that they didn't thank you. Or no one has acknowledged that you are such a great person for what you have done. All this makes you less likely to reach out and help them or someone else ever again because of that disappointment. Or what if your plan to do good isn't such a good plan and what you do doesn't work, but causes problems for the other person and they never want to speak to you again. And, you feel terrible.

Most of life's events are not wholly black or wholly white. They are shades of sepia with endless permutations and possibilities. And the fact that we are all more or less asleep at the wheel in the process of our gradual awakening into the light of inseparability means that our tendency to cruise along on a course of least resistance, where entrenched habits continue to be the most significant influence in our responses, results in us going along in the flow of the huge and miniscule life events with a limited set of emotions, conclusions, planned responses, and so on. Lacking much self-awareness or not having an ability to contemplate or meditate upon our life and circumstances, more than likely we will do what the adage I mentioned earlier says we shall do; perpetuate or build upon these events and our lives thus become more confusing and tangled. Although of our own making, our life literally spirals out of control. This is what lead a very wise Tibetan teacher to say that if we could live to be 1000 years old, but did not transform our minds and – in my words – recognize the beings of light that we are or have the potential to become, most of us would commit suicide at three hundred. We would be so laden with intractable habit patterns and the heaviness of accumulated emotion baggage.

REINCARNATION : God's recycling program

Clearly we do not seemingly have the capacities in these bodies to live to be a thousand years old. Instead, within roughly 100 years, most of us see the end of this particular incarnation. What happens next? Rather than go through the laundry list of interpretations from the various world religions, I would like to speak in succinct terms to the issue of reincarnation from my studies and experience in the conscious dying practices of Tibetan Buddhism.

From the deeds we have done in our lives, seeds are sown that have yet to break ground and blossom. How long does this take? If we look at life as a never-ending stream, how far downstream do the traces of our actions go? The answer to this last question is – in fact – endless. They don't stop. But obviously, in the current incarnation that we are in, we do.

This has to do with the future. But, where did the seeds sown before come from and how long ago were they coming to bring us into a body and mind that has had to deal with the ups and downs of this life here and now?

Because we are a part of the stream of existence inextricably connected to everything that vibrates and pulses in this universe, the beginning of which we cannot pinpoint, nor an endpoint, it would seem that chains of reactions that have brought us into this existence and the links we create in our own lives that connect us to the future make the conventions of birth and death that demarcate a time period in which we can identify ourselves as being us, is a concept at best; a snapshot of a flow unending.

If we stay with a strictly scientific approach and go with the understanding that energy is never destroyed, but only changes form, then this reasoning and the logic I have presented about karma and why we are where we are here and now, makes it reasonable to assume that notions of rebirth and reincarnation are altogether possible. That they are considered an abomination, a fairy-tale, just some new age hoo-hah according to modern-day Judeo-Christian theology has more to do with the political decisions that were made by in the early Middle Ages. In 325, the Council of Nicaea struggled with this issue and opted to create a strong church rather than strong people. The fact is, if you want to control people, it is hard to do so if they are a bit more relaxed and accepting of their fallibilities as humans and do not believe that this life is their only time or that they will go to heaven or hell everlasting depending on their compliance with the doctrine as interpreted by the power players of the day.

There is a popular conversation in any number of circles, new age, progressive, stoners sitting around, TV pundits taking the liberty to mock, where the question is asked, "Who was I in my previous life?" What is funny about this is that people have psychics or would-be fortunetellers or just their own self-talk telling them that they are from royalty, noble lineages of one kind or another. No one wonders if in their former life they were a garbage man or woodpecker.

For those of you who are either skeptical about the whole reincarnation thing or find it offensive to your religious upbringing, don't worry. You really don't have to believe any of this. A very renown female Tibetan teacher, herself recognized by her own community as a conscious reincarnate of a former teacher, keeps it simple and direct in a way that makes it easy for us all to be on the same page. She says that if you want to know who you were in a past life, look at where you are and what you are facing in your life now.

In the East, but also more and more in the West, the view on mind and consciousness from a scientific and philosophical standpoint is that it (mind) precedes body; that our thoughts determine how we work with the physicality of our bodies, and emotions are like a feedback mechanism between our thoughts and our bodies; i.e. the story we tell ourselves and others and the feelings we have about our story.

Anyone who has had more than one child knows that we are not – as was originally posited in our early sciences and philosophies – tabula rasa (blank slates) when born. We come in with a personality - a way of thinking and being all our own. Where does this come from? The mechanism that is described in eastern medicine and thought goes like this...

The habit patterns we have created from our actions and reactions to all that has happened to us in our lives creates a full range of body experiences, emotions, memories, and insights. When we die, there is no longer a body full of pain, our emotions become disconnected from the embodiment that registered happiness, sadness, anger, depression, and the like, so what is left is a consciousness of impressions and insights. What binds these to our body is our breath. This is not that far fetched if you think about dreams – where you can have memories, emotions, and experiences that are just contained by but are not being acted out through your body beyond neural activity. We also observe that if we are depressed or feel stressed out, our bodies feel tight, sore, and so on. But, if something happens to brighten our mood or lift our spirits, we breath deeper, relax more and – if we pay attention – notice that our body feels altogether different.

You will often hear from those sitting beside or reflecting on the death of a loved one, "Well at least they are now free from pain." This is not just a simplistic or hopeful wish. This is a reality. With the body now gone, the emotional or psychological antecedent to pain has no resting spot in the three-dimensional world in which to root. But, when our bodies are no longer in the loop, this mental energy doesn't just vanish. The truth is while thought and emotion is most noted by us through our bodies, there are so many examples we witness or experience where thought is faster than light. Think of the times when you think of someone and your phone rings and it is she or he. Coincidence? Or when a number of people have the same idea and do the same thing at the same time – what Ken Kesey called the "100th monkey effect." Disembodied thought linking with other similar thoughts – a group mind experience. Consider walking into a room where you can literally feel the emotions – like when we say the atmosphere was so thick with anger or sadness that you could "cut it with a knife."

The fact that the body dies and the breath ceases causes changes in our mental state, now moving towards disembodiment. This process is not immediate. We need to remember that there is still oxygen or life force in our cells and organs. There is a process that the mind is moving through here that is noted in Asian medicine, but also reported by those who master and have come back to tell us about the full death experience.

What is said and what I hold with faith at this point is that at some point in the death process, when the most significant point where the body no longer has the energetic capacity to hold the mind, that the separation between the two is like a force ten earthquake. Thus, unless the mind has been stabilized through rigorous meditation and contemplation, much memory of the life we are leaving is not retained by the mind. But, the momentum from karmic deeds, the energetic patterns of how our mind has worked and the strongest, most reinforced emotional patterns we have acted from in our lives persist. They put a "spin on the ball" as it were, directing us in a particular trajectory that eventually leads us, once again, into physicalizing and, once again, manifesting and playing out whatever insights and confusions we have from the habitual patterns of our mind's journey towards awakening.

Rebirth occurs when our parents-to-be make love. In their coming together, they create a vibratory pattern that, like a tuning fork or K-Mart blue-light special, attracts us back into incarnation.

New Agers like to say we chose our parents. Technically this is true. But, it is more like being compelled towards them reflexively. Although in the East there are those known as conscious reincarnates – those with extraordinary mind training and discipline from previous lives who can master the earthquake of death and move into another life so that they can bring more light into the world – most of us are on autopilot, cruising into our new existence habitually.

Depending on our state of mind, we shall end up in any number of circumstances. It was said by the Buddha that there are 84,000 kinds of beings, each dominated by a mix of emotions and clarity that are the direct results of previous activity and life responses. Thus we can end up in hellish or god-like states and a variety of other states in between. As a human, we may end up in the Hamptons or on the Riviera or Rwanda or the garbage dumps of Calcutta. But, then again, you could be a street person or wino in the Hamptons or an enlightened freedom fighter or progressive politician arising out of the garbage of Calcutta.

So many possibilities. All created by how we have responded to our previous life opportunities with intention and subsequent actions; all created as a platform for learning whatever it is we need to learn, however we need to manifest to help us mature our shard of awakening.

With this in mind, it stands to reason that everyone is doing their best based on what they know. We are all light and love in the process of awakening, whether we are a bird, a fish, a microbe (even Covid 19!), a god, or a human. Our progression to awakening depends upon whatever we can learn and practice that builds a mind and life that propels us towards greater moments of light and awakening. And it seems to me that such practices and the direction in which they lead builds a respect and kindness for each and every being. Our disregard, disconnection, belittlement, or indifference towards any being is an affront to creation and is a major roadblock that will – at some point – play itself out in the life that we shall eventually and inevitably step into.

This is not God's punishment. But, it is part of God's design. As beings of light not differentiated from light, we are given the endless opportunities for awakening to our potentials. How fantastic! We can screw up and end up in hells. We can do good things and end up in heavenly realms. But, depending on our responses to those situations, all can change. It all does. And once we awaken to this and understand the laws of the game, we become less the victim of our whims and more the masters of unimaginable potential, an unlimited mind, and great spontaneity and joy to play, celebrate, and shine for others – our brothers and sisters with whom we have never been separated.

We are here. We are going nowhere. And we are coming back. For there is nowhere to go and everyone who is around us, friend, foes, and strangers are all on the ride with us. Make them friends, be more inclusive, and the road becomes more joyful.

Because we do not have an enlightened eye to see how our actions and reactions to what happens in our lives is effecting us and others and where it is leading, most of us remain more or less unconscious in the process of our gradual awakening into the light of inseparability. For, in terms of life's circumstances, not having the ability to step back and see a far grander design at play, we see kind people or those who we deem good suffer or lead harsh lives and see scoundrels seemingly flourish with all that life has to offer. In what we erroneously perceive as a random world, we more than likely will find our minds and actions less guided by intent and mindfulness and compelled habitually to act randomly. This is especially the case in our relativized world where moral codes and behaviors of various traditions clash and compete and virtually negate themselves, allowing an amoral reality to surface as a viable option. Thus, our tendencies to cruise along on a course of least resistance becomes even more likely, ensuring that habits stay more entrenched and emotional baggage heavier. Rather than see the possibilities for change and transformation, we succumb to a view of ourselves based on the current circumstantial evidence which reinforces our view of being in charge, on top of it all on ones side of the spectrum and a victim of life's harsh realities on the other, with the various permutations between these extremes.

In describing the process of karma and reincarnation, I have made the case that what we do does matter and sets us along courses into lives and circumstances of our own creation. Upon more reflection and insight, if we knew what was coming next, perhaps we would not make the choices that we do. But, if it is also true that we do the best we can based on the current information that we have and our capacities in that time, how could it be any other way? Thus, when it comes to positive or negative, good or bad, white and black, when it comes to karmic seeds and deeds, how can we know better which is the best direction for us to go when it comes to our actions and reactions?

This brings me to the topic or concept of MORALITY.

Our Internal Moral Compass

As I have said a few times thus far, we all want to be happy. We don't want to suffer. This is true for each and every being. And, we notice that in the cultivation in deep and meaningful relationships, one of our greatest joys is seeing others who we care for in this life happy and more specifically when it comes to us in relation to them, happy with our behaviors towards and actions with them.

This is why in the teachings of the Buddha it is said that we are basically good and in my book, *The Passionate Buddha*, I speak of our *loving nature*. Despite all of the crime on the street and the wars in the name of this and that, we are lovers far more than we are fighters. Interesting fact: It was discovered that the rounds of ammunition shot during World War II far exceeded the number of casualties and that soldiers shot randomly more frequently than at another soldier. We can be trained to do this, but the training does have its consequences on our psyches, the subsequent quality of our lives and – yes - our karma.

Yet, because of the fact that we are immature in the truth of this loving nature that is us, codes of conduct have been established by groups of people to support individual and collective welfare and happiness. Such common sense has in turn become the foundations upon which various world religions have been built. I would contend that such religions have co-opted these common sense truisms or – in their attempt to posture themselves with some absolutist superiority – try to assert that the source of such is their own doctrine or the word of their particular deity as if beings trying to survive and lead happy lives had not thought of them already.

In general, whether it is the moral vows of a Buddhist monk or the Ten Commandments from the sons of Abraham, there are certain types of behavior and conduct that are generally encouraged:

1. Don't lie

2. Don't steal

3. Don't kill

4. Don't commit adultery or other such injunctions about sexual conduct

5. Don't be greedy or covetous over other people's stuff or relationships

6. In general, be respectful to your elders, especially your parents.

In most of my writings, I have said that we ALL know what is going on. We just agree not to blow each other's cover. In a similar vain, we ALL know what is right. Being beings of light, aspiring to live in that light and express our loving nature as demonstration of that light, we notice that if we pay attention, to decide to embrace and/or abide by such a code of conduct, we just feel lighter and happier. Things go easier, we are more relaxed, our relationships are more fulfilling, and we sleep better. We radiate a love for life. Conversely, when we ignore these things or try to get away with something less virtuous, there is "hell to pay." Even in the movies, if the story line depicts a cold-blooded killer, they are usually taking a break with a shot of whiskey, a nose full of cocaine, etc... Maybe this is just Hollywood, but I would find it hard to believe if a killer isn't always looking over his or her shoulder. Similarly, why is it that combat-hardened soldiers who have been trained to obey command and kill to survive or ordered to do so return to civilian life and struggle knowing that what they were asked to do they were taught at an early age was a sin and should not be done ever - albeit in a perfect world?

That our circumstances demand or we are called by others we chose to give our allegiance to do what we innately can feel to be against our loving nature has consequences measured not necessarily by how others view our actions, but by how the moral conundrum we have put ourselves in plays itself out in our minds and bodies. At the same time, the spiritual being that we are cries out and it is its relentless persistence as being the truth of who we are that often leads people in these circumstances to make decisions or act outside the bounds of convention; whether to take their own lives if the despair boxes them in with no sense of option, or breaking free of the conventions or the history they have lived thus far to embrace a higher or noble path on a road less taken; a path that others around them may not understand but is a testament to the fact that they have already traversed hell and high water. To find or rekindle your humanity, what would you do?

All of this is a testimony to the fact that whilst codes of conduct may need to be subscribed to as external supports to hold in and check behaviors and tendencies coming out of confusion, lust, greed, and the like, in truth we do KNOW better. We know and feel what works and what doesn't and when what is encouraged in these codes awakens within us what we innately feel in acting in such way, there is an alignment with the light of who we are that expresses itself outwardly in us being happy and radiating happiness to others. More to the point: These codes are within us. Our DNA resonates with the life giving and life affirming that comes from being guided by these conducts that makes us feel lighter in ourselves and promotes, enhances, and moves us ever closer to the awareness of God and the light of God that we are.

But, how does this look in our contemporary, materially based society?

We teach our kids to follow these codes, commandment, or injunctions. And yet, media and the culture we find ourselves in speak a message to the contrary.

Although in the movies the good girl or nice guy eventually wins, most of the plot and time in movies or TV shows is devoted to bad behavior and its rewards. There is no such things as joyful sex in the media. Sex is hot, lurid, sometimes dangerous or illicit, where the perfect looking guys and perfect looking girls bang away to really great music. The meanest, "cheatin-est" businessmen and women own the best houses and drive the coolest cars. And although the good guy may win, he or she probably drives away in a far modest vehicle. How boring.

Then there is our political landscape. In April 2012, twenty-nine members of Congress – those who represent us and swear to do our bidding - were looking at charges of domestic violence, seven had been arrested for fraud, eight had been arrested for shoplifting, and while debating on how to spend US citizens' tax dollars, 117 had bankrupted at least two of their own businesses.

(www.Snopes.com/politics/crime/congress.asp)

We tell our children they should not take drugs, while we drink martinis, take a hit, get anti-anxiety and anti-depressive meds from our docs and get them hooked on Ritilin because they are acting like children, which is what they are. The D.A.R.E program in the US is a failure, not because of peer pressure, but because we are a drug taking culture and parents model this by always modulating their own moods with one substance or another - prescribed, legal, or illicit.

And maybe when they are not on their own smartphone or media device, they catch a glimpse of the news, where world leaders are indicted for crimes against humanity, pay hush money to porn stars, priests are convicted of sodomizing little boys, where a Middle Eastern country drops shrapnel bombs on its own citizens, where drone strikes kill wedding parties, where corporations lobby to make their own companies exempt from legislation in case something goes wrong with their products, and a blind eye is turned to honor killings and public stonings of women who date outside their own faith or dare accuse men of a village of rape.

So, what does the moral landscape look like for our children? In such an atmosphere of hypocrisy, the gatekeepers of law and moral conduct have lost their

148

credibility either through their own immoral behavior or loss of absolutist authority. Thus, it only makes sense that if we are ever to bring back online a trustworthy and unshakeable reason for embracing moral behavior that we ALL know is truly what makes us happy, we need to take a serious look at all of our institutions and utilize media in a way that demonstrates the benefits and rewards of such behavior. A repentant change of behavior may be somewhat of use to restoring a smattering of confidence in a world spiraling out of control. In the long run and more directly to the point, though, for our collective future and to see something of worth come down the road, it is essential to re-direct attention through contemplation and mindfulness in our educational systems and at home. We need to awaken and fortify within ourselves and our children an awareness of the moral compass within each of us and encourage affiliations with others who wish to see the same in themselves.

If we are trained and encouraged to know who and what we are, we shall know how to be and what to do.

How we evolve or progress as individuals and what future awaits us is a direct result of who we have been and how we take and act on the light and dark of our beings up to this point and aim it towards the future. The chaos and cacophony of our current collective time on this planet is a symphony we have *all* created. It is our collective conundrum and as such, there is no part of what is in creation that we can ignore, discard, lust after excessively, or destroy that will not have repercussions for us all.

Years ago a Western Buddhist reincarnated lama from Canada, Namgyal Rinpoche talked about a future where mediocrity reigned and was marshaled over by draconian governments imposing rigid bureaucratic rules. In such droll and oppressive times, there would exist what he called "pockets of light;" communities of like-minded awakened people who would endure and pass on to future generations what was uplifting and useful for future generations. I shall discuss this further in the final chapter.

The image I have of a "pocket of light" community of individuals as envisioned by Namgyal Rinpoche is not a lock-step or unified card-carrying lot. In the multi-faceted world where there are so many options to deal with endless situations cascading continuously, if we learn how to discern through contemplation and meditation and have or embrace religions or spiritual paths that encourage us to trust and identify with the light from within and can see that light in the context of unfoldment and awakening into light, then the actions we take, whether they seem positive or negative based on the conventions of the day, will work out for the best for all concerned. As we are works in progress, what unfolds can never be perfect, especially if we are still stuck in a view of duality and trying to find perfect in the ever-moving target of manifestation. But, in circumstances where upliftment is the goal, the light that is shed may well infect us with a vision where the outer expression is just the joyful play of the stuff from which we have arisen and, as Lama

Ole says, we see that "everything is fantastic, just because it happens." That is: We are going in the best possible direction.

Although so much of what needs to happen for us to lead lives of love and light is an individual task, we need support and encouragement, and the discernment of those around us with a similar commitment. In this process, there will be or hopefully we shall meet some who are a little further down the road in their understanding and awareness who can hold up a lantern when our eye is caught in the darkness rather than the light and point us in a better direction.

This brings us to a discussion of the mentors, teachers, and leaders we encounter in both ordinary and extraordinary ways. Thus along with those we look to in our human family, I also want to discuss such beings in other realms of existence; i.e. lesser gods, Buddhas, saints, bodhisattvas, angels, nature spirits, and the like.

Chapter Six

Lesser Gods, Buddhas, & other beings in

Whom We Put Our Trust

There are realities that are invisible, imperceptible, or both.

Invisible implies that something is there, but we cannot see it. Because in our three-dimensionally fixated world we hold to the notion that "seeing is believing" - unless, of course you have a mental illness or you are on something that makes you see large white rabbits and so forth. Ruling these folk out, we tend to discount what people say or report that they "feel" about something if we ourselves cannot "feel" the same or are conditioned or encouraged to disregard such feelings.

Imperceptible implies that we have no perception, not even a feeling of something being there. Perception is attached to consciousness, hence more subjective by nature than the notion of invisibility. For example, it is said that native islanders did not see European boats in the water on the horizon, not because they were invisible, but because they had never seen anything like them. Their perceptions were not tuned into a way to frame what was there to be seen; hence, nothing was there.

Similarly, in the not too distant past, we use to watch people get sick and not seeing the viruses, microbes, and the like, concluded that sin, an evil spell, or curse was the cause of the malady. Of course, being science oriented we can now say that we "know" better. We can easily just shrug this off as superstition. But, as modern medicine begins to recognize what has been known for centuries in oriental medicine, i.e. the power of emotions and trauma on immunity, if you define a curse or spell as a powerful erroneous belief or shock, the impact of such emotional trauma coupled with lifestyle imbalances in diet and so on, there may indeed be a drop in immunity, we strangely give credence to the evil or "stink" eye. In keeping with the reasoning presented here, a mixture modern science, energetic medicine (i.e. Chinese Medicine and Ayurveda to name just two esteemed ancient healing systems), superstition, and belief systems have in 2020 and 2021 created a maelstrom of controversy, political debate, denial and fear cluster around a tiny virus, not unlike the many that have come, gone, and remain shrouded in confusion owing to the Three Poisons.

Science has also discovered that there are microbes living in unimaginably hostile environments, such as in the lava of volcanoes and in the ice of clouds. These little life forms have been named "extremophiles." Is it possible that ancient Inca or Aztec cultures sacrificing to the gods of the volcanoes or Hopi elders doing rain dances were serenading microbes to appease the roar of lava or beckon rain to come to their lands, respectively? I do not say these things lightly as I might have had I remained in my middle-class Jewish Midwest bubble all these years. But, alas, "that darned cat" also got out of the bag and will – like the other cats along the way - never return. That it cannot is not my mind just becoming hippie-fied or going soft. For, technology and science have been able to push the envelop and the spectrum of the visible and perceptible so many times over the course of history that I have no reason to doubt that we shall continue to stretch further, discover and establish as fact that which was once relegated to myth, insanity, or both.

At the same time, while science and technology may be able to explain or quantify, they may not improve how we interact with such forces; that we have a more scientific explanation, but still what works best is the forms of communication and interaction invented by our ancestors. I think of the time and energy devoted to developing contrails (Yes, they do exist and the US government officially acknowledged that they exist about seven years ago at a meeting held at the United Nations building in New york City.) to seed clouds for rain that yield little or opposite results, despite how well we understand the chemical properties of clouds. At more personal level, we can understand the biochemistry of attraction and love, but cannot bottle it or make any well-crafted product that compares to a little child reaching its arms out to be hugged.

And so I would like to share two short stories of why I have no problem with the Buddha's understanding that there are 84,000 types of consciousness, with most of them being invisible.

Shortly after I had been told this in a workshop in Woodstock, New York, my wife Melanie and I were living with her parents in her hometown of Hoddesdon, Hertfordshire, England. Melanie's blind and nearly deaf grandmother, Nana, also lived with Melanie's parent and had done so for years.

For the most part, Nana's presence in the house was peaceful. She had been there for years, tended tenderly by her daughter, Penny, Melanie's mother. Nana had a remarkable sixth sense for what was going on in the house. Despite being blind and deaf, she knew virtually everything that was going on throughout the house, even when Penny would have preferred that she didn't and often went to great trouble to not disclose anything to Nana about whatever she thought might excite or upset her. Still, Nana knew.

But, there were also times when Nana would ask why various people were in her room or the house when, based on the three dimensional world the rest of us were living in, there was no one to be "seen." This bothered Nana, but vexed Penny as she did not know what to do or how to respond to her mother's vehement claims. Was Nana losing her mind? Was Penny giving her mum too much medication?

Knowing that I had a counseling background, Penny asked me if I would talk to Nana to get to the bottom of the matter, I am certain that she had no idea what my line of query or comments would be.

Nana told me about the various visitors who came to her room. She did not seem distressed, but rather curious. Some of the visitors were people from her past who had died. Others were new to her. So, I told her about the 84,000 beings and their invisibility to the rest of us in the house. She smiled, reached out to grab my arm, sighed deeply and said, "What a relief." And from that point on she welcomed her visitors and enjoyed her time with them, leaving Penny mystified, but at least able to get on with other chores and activities in the house.

Was I just placating an old lady and her hallucinations? Or was this a reality? In my hospice work I have told any number of family members not to worry about whether their dying beloved was hallucinating or perceiving a different reality. The matter at hand is whether the visitations are helpful and bring solace or whether they are distressing. In this situation, the reality is trumped and defined by the relationship.

But, then there is this next story, which defies the hallucination rationale. This incident comes in the story of the passing of one of my daughters, Shamara Phillipa, from Sudden Infant Death Syndrome (SIDS) while a Buddhist teacher, Lama Ole Nydahl, was visiting us. The full account of Shamara's remarkable passing is in one of my books, *Rebirth Into Pure Land*.

In the evening after Shamara's passing and Lama Ole performing the transference of consciousness yoga, known in Tibetan as *phowa*, we held a meditation with several friends. At that time, my wife, Melanie, and I had an elaborate Buddhist shrine in the attic of the house we were renting in Lexington, Kentucky. On this shrine was placed an assortment of water bowl and food offerings to the Buddhas, bodhisattvas, dakas, and dakinis (gods and goddesses) which I replenished daily.

In the meditation that Lama Ole guided all through until late in the evening, he spoke of blessings from the Buddhas gently falling from the skies like snowflakes. Soon after he finished the meditation, our friends left and those who were spending the night in our house, including us, all went to sleep. Despite it being January, the night was warm and still.

I don't sleep much, so I was up early the next morning. As I looked out the window, I saw that the ground was covered in a fresh blanket of snow. Thinking of the previous evening's meditation. I was happy and amazed by this, even if it was just a coincidence. But, I was stunned to see that nearly half of the food and water that had been left on the shrine from the previous night was gone. We had no mice, no pets, and our kids who had gone to sleep early the previous evening were still asleep and knew better than to nibble off the shrine. My conclusion: The gods came and enjoyed themselves.

Since the passing of Shamara and the events of that evening, although I do not visually through my eyes see invisible beings, having witnessed what I witnessed in these events and witnessing in a similar way in other times in my life over the years, I have confidence – not faith, but confidence – that we are not alone and that there are many realms of existence in whose presence we make our homes, our neighborhoods, cities, and so forth. We are in the midst of a very populated universe with whom we can learn to communicate, cooperate, and thrive.

And, I would venture to say that each and every person reading this book could share similar stories, which, in the presence of those with whom you feel a kinship, I encourage you to share.

The point that we can communicate, cooperate, and thrive in relation to and with the help of many beings seen and unseen in our universe leads us directly into the discussion of gods, goddesses, Buddhas, gurus, and the like.

As I have stated earlier, I am a Buddhist, a student of the science of the mind as taught by the person in history known as the Buddha. As a psychological process of investigation, the teachings of the Buddha are non-theistic, a point which leads some to believe that Buddhists don't believe in God, that Buddha is a replacement for God, and other various distortions. In my case, as I have stated, I do have a faith in a creator god of which I am a part along with everyone and everything else. This is the god of Genesis that, I contend, gets badly represented or mistaken for some other gods or weird notions of who and what god is mentioned later on in the Old Testament.

For me, this god, this Creator, is found as both the sum and the parts of all that is manifest. Yet, this god is ineffable as well as omniscient, omnipotent, and omnipresent - no exceptions. What is seen as separate are but the shards of light of the great light that is this Creator God. And each shard expresses its light to a greater or lesser degree in the never-ending process of awakening to this Truth. Of course, some may want to qualify this by saying that this has to do with those who possess consciousness. And, indeed, as humans, we may be more comfortable with an anthropocentric view that we and perhaps animals and a limited number of invisible beings (i.e. ghost or gods) have consciousness that have the potential to awaken. In this matter, I think of the Manitou principle of Native Peoples who see each and every aspect of creation having spirit. As the mind science of Buddhism even posits that most of what I see from the limited view of three-dimensional perception is a phantasm that is self-created, I cannot be too sure that it is OK for me to disregard ANY aspect of what I see as having what Buddhists call Buddhanature; an innate capacity to wake up. Thus, how can I look up to some aspects of what I see or perceive and down at or be dismissive to other aspects?

There are some who know the truth of this well and those who do not. When there is a full recognition and experience of no separation, then such a being is fully awake. This is what is meant by the Sanskrit term "Buddha." The images that are depicted from the east as Buddhas are a representation of the internal state of awareness of such an "enlightened" being. The iconography is to depict what have been classically identified as the major and minor external and internal expressions of this awakened state. But we have gotten used to or become mistakenly convinced that a Buddha needs to look like a man in robes sitting cross-legged with hair tied up on the top of his head. However, there have been people who have woken up in all cultures in endless circumstances since the beginning of humanity. It does not mean that these people are different per se, but rather gifted with circumstances and capacities that support this awakening. Thus, an enlightened being for a Bushman from Africa may look completely different from an enlightened being in the eyes of a Tibetan Buddhist, a Christian, Muslim, or Native American. In the same way, seeing Jesus as an awakened being, I see no problem that the Scots and Irish have a red-haired pale white faced Jesus while Africans have a black Jesus, and Middle Easterners have a Semitic, Arabic looking Jesus who probably is most accurate in terms of Jesus as an historical personage.

From my studies and experiences, rightly or wrongly I perceive the Buddhas, the awakened beings in the seemingly infinite universes, as being educators, their job being to wake us all up to the truth of our inseparability with God and all things manifest. They have the instruction manuals on how to use consciousness most effectively to move it towards the light of awakening. This is NOT religious information or a slick multi-dimensional marketing plan to get you to buy into one reality, one version, some kind of cosmic in crowd. Dharma, as we have said, means the "way things are" and to add to this I would include the word "operationally." Such operational information will no doubt express itself in the cultures and idioms of the time. That some would like to claim exclusivity over this or that version is just a convention of the moment and circumstance. This is why it makes sense to me and see no contradiction in Trappist monks practicing Zen.

Buddhas understand how negative emotions veil or disguise the noble awakening qualities that we inherently are. Having transformed all of these, Buddhas are distinctly different from what are best described as lesser gods and demi-gods. Such gods are those who have come to some level of mastery over the world and their embodiment in such. Thus, they can live for extraordinarily long times and can have and sometimes even demonstrate their dominion over the elements and forces of nature in the world around us. However, because they still subscribe to a sense of a self separate from that which is around and within them, they are – like us – still caught in a state of alienation. Because their understanding is still somewhat limited, their actions are often tainted by negative emotional states - primarily pride and jealousy. And how many stories and myths exist in virtually all parts of the world and in so many world religions of how pride and jealousy creates the folly, foibles, and warring amongst gods? From such stories we – at best - we can learn important lessons of life.

Because Buddhas, gods, and demi-gods have achieved full or a greater sense of awakening to their full potentials, it makes sense to pay attention to them; to emulate their best qualities, ask for their help, seek and/or appreciate their presence.

Buddhas will help us to work with our potentials to go beyond the alienation of duality that keeps us tripping over ourselves and ending down more rabbit holes of

160

existences based on compulsions rather than clear choices. Once we have accomplished this, our presence is no longer determined by some internal drive or projection based on subconscious habitual patterns, but rather being in a state of awakened perfection. Our light is what is seen and envisioned by others similarly working in the same direction. An awakened being is said to have qualities that are a testimony to their perfection, but they appear to others based on the depth of awareness, sensitivity, and understanding they possess. That is why such beings are depicted in iconography in peaceful or wrathful, beautiful, or even hideous forms – all determined by the state of the mind of the being seeing them. This is no different from when we are in a bad mood and someone looks mean to us, or what they say is taken in a way that reflects our own projected confusion of the moment.

Gods, goddesses, and demi-gods and goddesses are useful. Because of their mastery over the phenomenal world, it is worthwhile cultivating a positive relationship with them. But, being just one more manifestation on the karmic soul train, it is better to entreat them and respect their dominions than worship them. They might enjoy you genuflecting, throwing your hard earned coins into the coiffeurs of their minions claiming to be doing their bidding. But such actions may increase their pride – something they don't need more of.

As humans, we feel most comfortable putting human forms and attributes on those beings we emulate, respect, even worship. Whether this anthropomorphizing tendency reflects who and what these Buddhas, gods, goddesses, and demi-gods and goddesses are or want, it is what we do in our process of trying to connect with them.

Based on this anthropomorphic tendency, our religious traditions encourage us to offer gold, silver, food or tangible goods to such beings. Offering what is precious to us does demonstrate our willingness to connect. But while this social convention has its usefulness, in the realm of humans, we build up expectations of a quid pro quo relationship; i.e. that what or how much we give should be reciprocated by whatever being we are lavishing. And then there is the comparing we do amongst ourselves, like if one devotee or parish member gives their guru or minister a Cadillac, another may feel compelled to offer a Rolls Royce.

When it comes to relating and showing our respect to Buddhas, our greatest appreciation is demonstrated through our willingness to learn and test out what they offer. Buddhas don't want card-carrying, blind-faith followers. They want compatriots; compatriots of light, living in the truth of our inalienable state. In such a world, there is no part of God's creation that is higher or lower in potential. Thus looking down or belittling an ant is a denigration of that which we are a part. When fully awakened, we know this to be true. That is why it is natural for awakened beings to show respect, love, and compassion for all regardless of stage or stature.

That gods and goddesses may want you to feel lower than them is just their problem. And for you to feel lower or lesser than them is yours. For in truth, what is most beneficial for them is for you to show a respect for their accomplishments and utilize the resources they offer and/or honor dominions they master. For example, to show respect and make an appropriate and worthy offering to the Lord of the Sea, Neptune, Poseidon, or whatever name you may give them, you don't pour your sewage into the streams, rivers, lakes, and oceans or senselessly slaughter fish or torture them by cutting off their desired body parts and dumping them back into the sea to suffer. To gods of the land and mountains and forests, you don't scatter your garbage, greedily extract the earth's minerals and fluids, leave toxic radiation tailings on the lands for animals to become poisoned, or uproot flora and fauna or spray it with chemicals in a way that shows a wanton disregard, hubris, or sense of entitlement. If the God of which we are a part has truly said that we are stewards of his creation, so far we are doing a rather poor job and are not holding accountable those who rape this beautiful planet for their own pleasure and greed. Thus whilst in creation there are natural environmental and ecological shifts and changes, is it possible that when we make matters worse through our own ignorance and disregard, that in response or defense, the lords whom hold dominion over such forces and realms act in kind? Is it mere superstition or primitive thinking to think that when the seas roar and the land cracks and shifts, when there are floods and famines that those who hold dominion are acting to re-establish the balance that we have upset?

My sense is that what all such gods and goddesses, demi-gods goddesses and other beings connected to elemental forces of the natural world ask of us is that we recognize our connection and inter-dependence with nature and demonstrate a mindful respect so necessary for a sustainable and thriving eco-system.

Pray to Poseidon, Apollo, Osiris, Ahura Mazda, Yahweh, Allah, sun and moon gods and goddesses. Invite pixies to your gardens and pray to the fairies in the trees. You won't hear complaints from gods and the like if you pray and lavish them with all sorts of wonderful gifts and offerings. But, without following up by paying attention to the natural elements to which they are masters and servants, your prayers and offerings will just be a waste of time and resources. When you are smashing your own head with a mallet, there is no point in praying to a god to take away your headache. When you build ticky-tacky houses in America's Tornado Alley, there is no point in blaming God if your house gets demolished. If you eat chemicalized dead food, there is no point in asking God to take away your cancer. Without your efforts, your prayers amount to nothing more than complaints and an abdication of your personal responsibility for your part in creation.

The "my will versus thy will" conundrum so often uttered with disempowering piety is an artificial construct rooted in alienation. Once you develop a deeper understanding and appreciation of the inter-dependence of all things, you understand that your full participation in life is the shortest path in overcoming the existential and spiritual dilemmas you beat yourself up with, in which case the will and joy you apply to what you do becomes a positive contribution to your awakening and the betterment of all.

If we understand that we are a part of and not separate from creation as the creator itself, turn to those who can instruct us to wake up to this realization, honor the guidance and resources of those who show mastery over the creation that we share and are one with, and support all other life forms in a way that shows respect and care, **then we are living and integrated, functional, spiritual life.** And all gods, goddesses and Buddhas, all fairies, elves and pixies, all devas, dakas, and nagas will rejoice.

In the scheme of what I am presenting here, each transcendent, visible or invisible being to whom we ascribe a name or title of significance has their part to play. And like all sentient life, they all want to be happy and live a life free of suffering. They are each either identified with and awakened to that which they are a part – just like us – or seek in their own way the realization of such. Thus whilst they are not equal or the same in their realization, awareness, or capacities, that they are not is irrelevant and does not make our worship or appreciation of them lesser than some other approach. In this way, faiths or traditions that connect with particular enlightened or powerful beings and forces have something to contribute to a world where inclusivity and the shared goal of awakening for the benefit of all and fostering one peaceful and thriving world becomes the focus. Whereas science and technology may reveal the substance and mechanism at play, what makes life worth living and joyful is relationship. Thus, that there are traditions which over the ages have developed practices, prayers, and rituals intended to cultivate sacred and transcendent relationships with such beings cannot be discounted as a vital feature and potent force for effecting the positive changes we seek in the world today. After all, we are certainly in this all together. We need all hands on deck. Why settle for ordinary when we have those amongst us who may have knowledge on how to employ the powers and gifts of the extraordinary?

In this regard, an important step along the way is to become more comfortable in each other's presence; to break bread and even pray with those whose faiths are different from our own. We are living in a time when we all see the pain and suffering brought about by exclusivity, chosen people claims, and holier than thou action. Beyond such awareness and a call for tolerance, I think that we are in a time when the calling together of beings ordinary and transcendent would not only be welcome or refreshing. I think it is a vital step in the path of awakening in a Free World.

Am I asking something that is preposterous? Only from the perspective of us as humans with the habitual tendency towards exclusivity and wanting to be on the right/winning/most divine side. For in fact, in the Tibetan Tantric tradition that I have practiced for over 40 years, there are deep and powerful meditations where Buddhas, gods, elemental forces, even demons are called upon to work together. On the level of the transcendent, the invisible realm or spectrum we are only separate from by virtue of awareness or lack of, there is no problem here. Thus, if the Buddhas, the gods and such can do it, shouldn't we - as part of our practices and devotions to them - follow suit?

For some who read this, you still may have your issues with gods and/or notions of transcendent or invisible beings. No worries. If you pay attention to developing mindfulness and try to maintain a healthy regard for the world around you, it doesn't matter if you believe or not. Embracing life-affirming metaphors and empowering archetypes and ecological and inclusive conceptual frameworks will do. What matters most is that your actions based on whatever inspires you in an Ecology of Oneness way will accomplish what is needed. And with a peaceful heart aligned to the betterment of all, when we come to the end of our days, each of us will find out the truth of all of this anyways.

Teachers, Priests, Guru, and The Folks We Trust

Before we embark on the matter of the many teachers, priests, gurus, shamans, and other wise folk who we often place our spiritual trust in, I want to make one thing perfectly clear.

You don't need to be saved.

No matter how bad, confused, bereft, or messed up you think you are, no matter what you think, whatever you say or do that is in contradiction to your inherent loving nature –NONE of that is you. Whatever runs counter to the awakening potential within each and every one of us are reflexive, reactive, subconscious patterns rooted in the Three Poisons of ignorance, attachment, and aggression. They are only you insofar as they are the alienated you struggling with the self-contrived demons that merely reflect the process of awakening that arises in the labyrinth your being-ness walks to reveal its true nature. And whilst there may be friends and helpers along the way who need to seduce you from the dark side, stop you in your tracks, perhaps even temporarily take you out of the misery you inflict upon yourself and others, in the end, the only person who is going to save you is you. And, if anyone claims that it is their responsibility or calling to save you, they are either a mistaken fool or a charlatan. But to be fair, when we are so very disconnected from our being, that we project for ourselves something or someone outside of ourselves that we then label as the cause of our salvation, does have a usefulness when the habit patterns seem so solid and intractable. And in this lifetime, that may be as good as it gets. But, in the long-term journey of our being

167

towards awakening, such reliance will have to be discarded. Otherwise, it will become stifling and possibly introduce us to other ways in which distraction and alienation manifest. It becomes like, as a fellow therapist once said about addiction, changing rooms on the Titanic.

That said, I remind you of my dedication to my teacher Kunzig Shamar Rinpoche and the adage that a good teacher is someone who rows you to the other shore, then burns your boat.

Although teachers, ministers, priests, gurus, shamans, elders, and the like are usually neither invisible or imperceptible, as they are in front or known to us personally or by reputation, we turn to them as embodied or study their lives, works and words for guidance, inspiration, support, and/or reinforcement examples. As such they can be tremendous sources of inspiration. But, in these days of media and transparency of public figures, they can also be sources of the destruction of our confidence in anything spiritual through their excesses in power and inappropriate sexual behavior.

Let's start first with my concluding observation about those to whom we go to for spiritual inspiration and support.

In the inter-dependent universe that I am describing, we are endlessly and ongoingly surrounded by sources of inspiration. In fact, ANYTHING and ALL THINGS can be this way for us; a baby smiling at us, a car crash, a bird in flight. In fact, it is said in the Buddhist tradition that if we can mindfully pay attention and immerse ourselves fully in the act of sneezing, we can wake up.

Because we mostly live with a dualistic headset of alienation, the miracles of everyday common occurrences don't do it for us. Not embracing the possibilities in our true potentials, we search outside ourselves for what will make us feel complete. And as a species who are social and loving in nature, we look around us. Some may look to the beauty of nature or their pets. But, for the most part, we turn to each other; others who are like ourselves, but whom we presume are better or have it more together than us. And from their guidance and/or example, we venture to make ourselves better – inevitably striving to heal the illusion of separation that is at the core of our suffering. The dilemma of this approach is that the act of reaching out in such a way, in an act of longing, desperation, bespeaks the problem we are trying to solve.

In the vision of a free world sustained by the Ecology of Oneness, if any teacher is worth their salt, their only purpose should be to support us in the healing of the illusion of separation by directing our inquiry and longing back to the inherent potentials within us. Thus first and foremost, you don't want to find a teacher whose focus is on making you a follower or fold member. You want to find someone who from the outset sees as their task you becoming you and not a version or reasonable facsimile of them. In the spirit of Oscar Wilde, the message is "Be yourself. Everyone else is already taken."

A teacher, priest, or master who has as teaching as his or her primary function can appear in so many ways. If you feel confident in their character and style, they may well offer techniques of transformation that each of us would benefit from learning. With that said, however, as a general rule, I think it is useful to find teachers and the like whose life is not that different from your own or is a model for how you want to live. Thus, if you are married or in a relationship – or want to be – it makes little sense to talk to a celibate priest or monk about your sex life or relationships unless they have been in such and perhaps are just in a new stage of life for reasons other than running away from such. The same goes for family life, the raising of children, holding down a job, even military experience if that is your background. Priests who struggle with their sexuality make poor relationship counselors. Siberian shamans can tell you little about how to manage your financial affairs in the Bay area. As such, the teachers who offer you advice and guidance should offer that which supports your lifestyle if such goals are part of how you see yourself. In my own case, I know how tormented my wife, Melanie, was in the early years of our relationship with Tibetan Buddhism. The aspiration lamas encouraged us to aim for was doing a three-year retreat with other committed devotees. Many of our friends did such with disastrous results for their families. Fortunately for us, as we moved along our life together, I realized how precious our relationship was as a path of awakening in and of itself. At this stage of my life, I feel that whilst a retreat could be useful, I no longer have the desire to subject anyone to this choice and feel blessed in the love and transformational power of the marriage to my Beloved that I celebrate every day.

Similarly, there are stories of the beatified, the saints and transcendent masters and such whose lives are more often than not recorded in such a way as to emphasize the miracles that such beings may or may not have performed. As I have witnessed miracles in the presence of living masters, I have no reason to doubt such accounts. However, what is more important to me is the context and actions they took in their lives as spiritual beings going through the human experience. Rather than only hearing the sanitized version of their lives, I want to know how they were as children, what was their relationship with the parents, and the trials and tribulations they had to endure and transcend. This gives me more to work with than knowing that they could turn water into wine.

For years I have shared with friends and students that I am looking for the "Ozzie and Harriet" Buddhas. For those of you unfamiliar with 1950's American television sitcoms, the "Ozzie and Harriet" TV show was about the Nelson family. The dad, Ozzie, owned a hardware store, and Harriet was a housewife, cooking, cleaning, taking care of their teenage boys, David and rock star singer, Ricky. They paid their taxes, were upstanding members of their community, and rolled with whatever dilemmas and antics two teenage boys could throw at them, especially their heart-throb teen idol, Ricky, to whom Ozzie would often offer wise counsel along the way, which he, Ricky, always found was the best course of action. More or less ordinary folks, committed to each other, trying to be good, honest, decent, caring people. In an age where relationships are tenuous or strained, the schism between the generations vast, and a the pursuit of material acquisitions trumping decency, the fictitious life of Ozzie and Harriet as archetypes of modern day worldly Buddhas seems appropriate and worth aspiring to. In these days, I want to expand my vision to say that Ozzie and Harriet could be beatified for living the miracle of healthy, simple, engaged, and compassionate lives.

In the melting pot world of colliding social, cultural, and religious realities, you may find that a Hindu priest, Buddhist Rinpoche, high wiccan priestess, or Native American elder is the guise such a teacher takes for you – despite your Judeo-Christian, Western cultural background. In a state of alienation, we often feel alienated from identifying with let alone see examples of others within our own milieu who are more than likely there, but whom we cannot see. Thus we get attracted to the seemingly exotic or foreign. It allows us to temporarily by-pass the aversion we have for the skin we are in and the circumstances of our daily grind.

An alternative explanation to this also exists which I feel compelled to express as it is at once true and a part of my story in our melting pot world.

As we are constantly recycling into existence from previous embodiments, we end up in a new skin, sex, culture, and so on, yet have strong karmic ties to other cultures and ways we have been a part of in previous lives. This may, similarly, compel us to identify with what may seem so foreign to ourselves or others. Again, in the case of Melanie and myself, in our adult lives we have always felt more comfortable amongst Indians, Nepalese, and Tibetans despite the fact that up until the writing of this book, we have never travelled to the East in this life. And, we have doctors and high masters stay with or visit us who comment that our mannerisms and how we live is reminiscent of an Indian or Tibetan way of life. But, as we have grown in our own spiritual development and awakening, we have

172

become more comfortable in our whiter skin on the central coast of California. Rather than deifying or reifying our distant Tibetan and Indian roots, we find ourselves seeing in the many and diverse cultures, people, and circumstances around us examples and lessons that inspire us and transcend karmic patterns that we have heretofore identified with. And thus we are as comfortable with a Hindu ashram or Buddhist meditation hall as we are praying in a temple or church, or – in my own case - attending meetings as an officer in my local Masonic lodge.

Thus, regardless of whether your path from alienation to awakening sees you staying within your own church, heritage or culture or being attracted to what is foreign from either alienation, karmic links, or both, if the teaching and guidance you receive is truly beneficial, you should notice that the field of possibilities for awakening and embracing the world and those around you grows and the sources of inspiration expand infinitely. Conversely, if the opposite takes place, where you find yourself shrinking away, limiting your contacts to an echo chamber of only those whose views and belief are like your alone – then the gift and possibility of awakening in the Free World is lost – at least temporarily.

For all times, but – as we are here and now – especially in our times, a good spiritual teacher or mentor should embody and be a support for you to fall in love with the world- the world that you have never, ever been a part of from. And this love is not a love of sentimentality. It is a love of compassion, intelligence, and strength. As such, how you live in the world, whom you affiliate with, and how you contribute to the further uplifting of the world and all within it eradicates your role as the victim in your own life or the servant of another – which amounts to one and the same thing. At this point, the teacher is no longer a teacher. They become a witness – a witness to celebrate the light that you are, the shard of God that is you, shining. And the role of the teacher is done, because the student is now the teacher.

And, as a teacher, in the days to come, you become a beacon to support those who are attracted to and can grasp the significance and responsibility it takes to infuse the world with the Oneness vision that supports harmony, peace, and transformation – regardless of whether we see it before our eyes or not.

Chapter Seven

Spiritual Practices and Disciplines:

Critical Thinking and Transforming Your Inner landscape

In several of my previous books I have discussed in length the steps and stages of various forms of meditation. Thus, if you want to learn those techniques I encourage you to look at those works.

While each one of the techniques I have shared has as one of its key components, mindfulness, I would like to mention this concept here on its own. For mindfulness has become a buzzword in psychotherapy as being synonymous with meditation without religious or spiritual overtones. It is also bandied around in marketing and media to elevate otherwise trivial ideas and concepts to levels of seeming sophistication.

In order to de-mystify meditation, prove its overall usefulness for human development, and – for those who it matters to - allay people's fears that meditation is an Eastern religious "thing," effort has been made in the neuroscience and psychotherapeutic community to talk about mindfulness and mindfulness techniques as either the primary component, if not the entirety of what is meant by meditation. Nevertheless, with a focus on this component, brilliant research has been done using neuroscience and biofeedback to verify measureable changes in brain and body chemistry and physiology. And, along with the measureable benefits of such "mindfulness" practices from a scientific point of view, there have been testimonials and commentaries of those reporting how their lives have been changed for the better as a result of their practice of mindfulness.

Many of the mindfulness-based techniques focus singularly on reducing stress and positively affecting the state of the body and mind of the one practicing them. This is a good first step for many. But, I contend that for these techniques to be truly beneficial, there needs to be willingness to tap into human altruism, our loving nature, and thus encourage an awareness that brings the person into an intimate awareness of their inter-connectedness with all that is around them and how their mindfulness can be employed as a tool for making more affective anything and everything they do. Within this framework, the concept of critical thinking skills as emphasized by Tibetan Buddhist master, the Venerable Kunzig Shamar Rinpoche, is most apropos. If one takes the word critical not to mean something like being a criticizing annoyance, but rather critical as in "critical mass" where a point is reached in the development of something that brings it into fruition, then we have mindfulness shaped by wisdom and skill leading to balanced, effective action. If mindfulness does not lead to such, what is its point anyway?

In this light, education and contemplations that fill in the picture within the frame of mindfulness is crucial to make it more than just a mind-body stress reducing experience. There needs to be a moral framework. In an earlier chapter I have written at length about our inner moral compass; that we do, in fact, know what is good and wholesome in thought and action. Within the context of meditation, I am suggesting that for mindfulness to be truly effective, it needs to be guided by intentions that arise from our loving nature as revealed to us by this inner moral compass. As mindfulness and self-awareness support an experience of our inner moral compass, in a culture that does not encourage these qualities, it does make sense to avail ourselves of the prescribed laws or codes set down by elders from our past that encourage to take heed, especially when circumstance or habit compels us to act otherwise. As we do this and continue to practice mindfulness, what inevitably begins to occur is that that which was externally encouraged, becomes internally revealed, at which point mindfulness supports morality and visa versa.

Morality may seem such an old fashioned or heavy-handed notion – like when someone moralizes at us in ways that diminish the complexity in our everyday actions to black and white components. Whilst guilt-ing someone into not making heinous mistakes or committing a deed that harms self or others has its place, I think of this as a last resort – a morality of necessity. Sadly, within the normal range of human action, I think because morals are often thought of as restrictions of freedom, thus punishment, many of us would like to hear the truisms that morality represents as infrequently as possible. In the material world where most erroneously place their faith and refuge, it seems that greed and deception are readily rewarded. In the eyes of the convention of the time, nice guys may be the guys we want to live next door to, but they finish last when it comes to the successful acquisition of the toys we are encouraged to strive for.

In truth, morality is about what works at creating the greatest joy and most freedom for all. It is interesting to note that in Buddhist philosophy, there are six virtues that are extolled. All of them together – generosity, kindness, discipline, patience, meditation, and wisdom – create what could be called a moral life. However, the word that stands out in this list is *discipline*. The Tibetan for this term is *tsultrim*, which, interestingly enough, also implies if not means *joy*. These two words, discipline and joy, seem so far apart in definition and yet there is a logical reason why they fit so well together. Taking a simple example: Everyday you get up and it is one of the disciplines to beginning your day to brush your teeth. Initially, you are taught this and of course when we are just learning, we resist. Yet, over time the discipline of doing this every day upon waking begins to pay off as we notice that our mouth just feels better when we do it. And, we notice that when we don't do it, we feel out of sorts – like something is missing. The act of brushing one's teeth as creating happiness or joy may seem like a stretch, so let's think of other actions where ongoing practice yields a result where there is a sense of lightness, ease, and satisfaction – all aspects of what I think of being a part of joy. Beyond the discipline of hygiene, consider eating regular meals, keeping one's space clean, changing your own motor oil, attending to your pet's welfare, the needs of children and others, defending one's country, mastering a challenging task and the feelings that arise form performing that task well. And from the ongoing consistency of such actions, joy naturally arises.

In the process of awakening, our habitual patterns rooted in the Three Poisons of ignorance, attachment, and aggression breed resistance and reluctance. We just want to do what we want to do. It is generally true that whilst there are volumes upon volumes of wise teachings and the presence and opportunity to connect with

178

teachers and others who could help us with the work of bringing out our best, what shakes us up to begin to change this situation is more often than not one form or another of disaster; an illness, a death, or some other traumatic event of which we are the focus or a part. Medically speaking, after a personally traumatic event such as a heart attack, where one has been fortunate enough to be involved with an integrative medical model, mindfulness practices are introduced. And patients learn to deal with, if not reverse the symptoms of their disease. The problem we face when disaster is our motivator is that when things begin to settle down or ease off, most of us will slip back into the patterns that are most comfortable for us, not realizing that we are courting the possibility of other such events in our future. At some point, we have to wake up to the fact that we are *never off the hook*! As the Venerable Tarthang Tulku has said, "Life exacts a price for less than full participation."

If we are one of the fortunate whose minds naturally turn to the light or are one of those who a slap up the side of the head has been necessary, "The Four Thoughts that Revolutionize the Mind" can be a great inspiration and/or motivator. This four-step process from the Tibetan Buddhist tradition looks at our human condition in a holistic and all encompassing perspective, concluding that waking up and being fully present in life is the essential task of our lives. As I write to friends not infrequently, "Shine! What else is there to do?"

The Four Thoughts begin with an appreciation of what is called "Precious Human Birth." Historically, this had to do with having a fully intact body and mind, with all parts working and all senses functioning in a place and atmosphere where peace and harmony encouraged learning and growth. With respect to our bodies and minds, there are now prosthetics that can replace damaged or lost limbs, organ replacements, more and more devices to enhance our senses of seeing, hearing, and touch if damaged. In a world where there are fewer and fewer places where isolation is possible, people in dire circumstances know of other possibilities through media and contact with others not entrenched or fully caught up in the dramas and traumas of the locale. And there are those who overcome the odds of such circumstances by force of will or heartiness of spirit. Thus, more and more there is the possibility of appreciating the preciousness of our human existence; another example of a freer world. And, the bottom line really has to do with where we are at within ourselves. Consider Helen Keller. Consider Nelson Mandela. Consider unsung heroes who live spirit-inspired lives despite the external definitions and expectations, which would otherwise define their situations as hopeless.

But, no matter how perfect or challenging a precious human birth may appear, it is, like all things, impermanent.

This quality of impermanence is something that looms as ominous and sobering in a world obsessed with a youth culture fearful and in denial of the truths of dying and death. I do not think that this is a wholly modern phenomenon. We like to maintain, protect, and preserve our lives, the lives of those around us, and what we have around us. That we do so seems reasonable if it is done with a sensitivity to the instability and ever changing nature of life as we come to see it pass before our eyes. But, what is this ongoing tidal process actually revealing to us?

Indeed, we are whizzing through time and space, arising and dying continuously on a cellular level. And yet we are beings of light, more space than matter, never truly separate, never truly alone. And that which is the vehicle or vessel that reveals this nature to us has at this time a human appearance. That it does has a cause, something that we are participants in creating. For right now, how well are we using what we have? How can we use the tools and potentials that we have here and now to fully embrace the majesty of the God of which we are not separate and help others to do the same? And as this vehicle moves through time a space, can we do so with grace and ease rather than resistance and the terror that comes from our confused attempts to make things stay as they are or want them to be in spite of realities to the contrary?

The third thought to consider builds on the first two. Indeed, your life is precious and, at the same time, impermanent in its physical expression. There is nothing you do that does not have consequences in the ongoingness to your life and what you experience. As mind always precedes and is the causal factor in our bodily expression, working with the transformation of our minds to identify with our loving nature is that which continuously rewards us with greater joy, bliss, and possibility. And because we are embodied, we need to understand the mechanisms by which we can most efficiently use our current potentials to ensure this transformation stays as the focus of our lives. Thus knowing how to take care of our bodies through diet, exercise, relaxation hygiene, hydration is both logical and necessary. Of course, our minds are so amazing that we can learn to adapt to and work with almost any situation to awaken. But if we could, would we not want to live healthier, stronger lives to make the work of awakening more harmonious and peaceful? Furthermore, in an inter-dependent world, does it not also make sense to make efforts to create the same for others?

The laws of karma, of course, do not require that this is what is available to you. Indeed, what you need to awaken may be a world of nuclear devastation and desperate people who want to take what you have and kill your family along the way. The fact is that we never experience anything that we are not consciously or subconsciously co-creators of. Thus, the laws of karma ask us to step up to the plate of our lives; to fully participate and become "response-able." Masters or victims, the tools are still in our hands. What do you want it all to look like? Here is where discipline and joy prove themselves inter-dependent.

Based on understanding these three thoughts, it would seem wholly beside the point and a waste of time if we were not to do all we could to awaken fully to the majesty of our life and the beauty of the world of which we are a part is. This is the fourth thought. Based on this logic, what else is there to do if we truly want happiness?

With such an appreciation for what we have here and now, mindfulness becomes more than just a tool for us to just feel better. It becomes a tool that yields its rewards not from the elimination of symptoms of stress, but by awareness that expands our vision. We are more understanding of who and what we are and have and see it within the context of a world from which we are never alienated and which responds to any and all acts of us expressing our loving nature.

It's not about you, but you are included

As I have repeated several times throughout this book in one way or another, inherent in our lives as beings of light not separate from God is a loving nature. Although out of ignorance, attachment, and aggression, the Three Poisons, we may be at times more or less "me"-centric, our greatest joy and contentment comes from seeing the joy and contentment we support in the lives of others. Acts where we demonstrate generosity, kindness, patience, where we know when to be quiet or step forward in another's life – such skills and actions open us more and more to the truth of our inalienable state.

Consequently, spiritual practices and disciplines should implicitly in their promise of uplifting our lives, lead to a state of being that not only inform, inspire, and transform us, they should similarly be the cause for us opening up to the world to effect the same in the lives of each and every being we touch. To accomplish this, these practices should help us overcome our erroneous sense of individuality over and above the universal collective. Modern philosopher, Tim Freke, speaks of transforming and transcending the singular prison of individualism to the wholistic awareness of our inseparability with all in the very ecological sensibility of Oneness. He speaks of us becoming "*unividuals*," a word I dearly love.

Please note here how I structure what I am expressing here. That you are who you are bears your originality, your self-generated uniqueness, but only as a juxtaposition of time and space and the meaning and purpose that drives your life based on the sum total of your experiences since beginningless time in an interdependent universality. This is a rather dry way of telling you that the love you extend to others around you **includes** you. That is why author Stephen Levine speaks of showing our selves mercy and Dr. Darren Weissman of the LifeLine Technique states that self-love is the greatest healer.

Thus, if your love for humanity and others is based on a martyrdom paradigm where self-loathing and/or self sacrifice is born out of a sense of you being a sinner, please stop. Give yourself a break. Give others a break as well. And if you can't help yourself, seek help, preferably with a kind, self-loving therapist or priest who demonstrates in their character a sense of self-love and acceptance.

Deepening Your Journey

In a culture that seems almost schizophrenic in wanting to claim a scientific sophistication while shying away from the latest discoveries in quantum physics and other sciences that are daily verifying the reality as expounded by mystics and sages in our human history, many of have sought answers to the deeper questions of life elsewhere. Rooted in a materialistic perspective and dismissive of the invisible world and forces that most of us feel one way or another over the course of our lives, such a model leaves us existentially dissatisfied and spiritually bankrupt. Religious institutions focusing on power and influence for some version of "greater glory" have relegated to almost extinction esoteric wisdom that encourages spiritual growth and development. In the Judeo-Christian paradigm, this wisdom is there, but often jealously concealed or fragmented if discovered. Thus, many have found solace and sustenance in Eastern traditions, where the esoteric remains relatively in tact and accessible. But, as I have said at various points, familiarity with these traditions and the cultures from which they have come has eventually led many to see that corruption and misuse of ecclesiastic authority and wisdom for power, influence, and satisfaction of more base and selfish purposes is almost as commonplace as with the traditions close to home we have come to disdain.

Nevertheless, it is clear that the traditions of the East have stayed more in touch with not only the mindfulness practices of basic contemplation and meditation, but also more advanced methodologies for spiritual awakening and maximizing specific qualities we can use to better serve our world; wisdom, compassion, protective activity, and so forth. And just as mindfulness-based meditation has now gained credence in scientific and medical circles, the psychological, emotional, and spiritual transformation available through the more advanced methods from Buddhist and Hindu tantra, and the upsurge in interest in the mystical teachings of Gnostic Christianity, Sufism, and Kabalistic Judaism, Theosophy, Masonry, and yoga to name just a few are being proven through insights into the inner workings of the universe and our minds found in quantum physics, epigenetics, and neuroscience. Spirituality and science together – centuries in the making.

Before I elaborate on this meeting of science and spirituality, I want to make a point, which I feel is essential if the deeper spiritual practices of the world's wisdom traditions are to act as an evolutionary and transformational tool in the chaos of our Free World.

Years ago, when training with Dr. Lobsang Rapgay, a clinical psychologist at UCLA and former religious secretary to His Holiness the Fourteenth Dalai Lama, he presented a schematic of the layering in Buddhist tantric spiritual practice. To my mind, this schematic applies to every tradition, East and West.

When people at first express an interest or desire to connect with a spiritual tradition to help them in their lives, the path presented is often very peaceful and calming. Prayers, contemplations, and meditations that focus on peace, joy, equanimity, and belonging ground us, settle disturbing emotions, act as a balm for harsh memories, and so forth.

But as we settle into the state of ease that hopefully results, subconscious patterns of negative emotions and behaviors begin to come up to the surface. As habits well reinforced over time, the new peaceful mentality or consciousness we are attempting to live in are confronted by the old patterns of anger, jealousy, frustration, sadness, pride, and so forth. The shadow emerges, subverting our noble ambitions and drawing us into a world of drama so often experienced in religious communities.

In traditions with access to or still practicing the full gamut of wisdom gleaned at the level of the intuitive esoteric, there are practices specifically designed to address the habitual and subconscious mind and all of its patterns and games. This is where spiritual practice gets serious and deep. Feeling the pain of negative emotions, being self-reflective and honest about one's experience, one faces these obstacles

186

and issues as opportunities. In Buddhist tantric meditations, the visualizations of meditation deities go from the peaceful, white, and beautiful images of early practice to wrathful, fierce images that confront us and move us forward. That is what is needed. It is hard and often painful work to uproot that which is the source of why you feel stuck.

When it comes to engaging a spiritual practice at this depth, a firmer commitment is essential. My recommendation is that if you have such a practice, stick with it. At this level, there is nothing much to be gained by mixing and matching practices and traditions. This may be interesting as an intellectual exercise in appreciating that other traditions may have what your tradition has. It may enrich your path and give you a greater appreciation. But that's about it. Thus although I am encouraging for people to experience each others spiritual practices, join in ritual, break bread and so forth, this level of the spiritual journey is very personal and guidance from those who have gone before, essential.

Such spiritual practices are rooted in the various esoteric traditions in the world. And as such, there is often some level of ecclesiastic baggage that comes along for the ride. This may act as a deterrent for some to engage in that which they may not be ready for. But, sadly it also acts as a turn-off as the less savory dimensions of religious association and participation are anathema to the true freedom and awakening that such practices often result in. And that is why the discoveries in the sciences and therapeutic methods of today are an exciting alternative and present possibilities for transformation once only possible in more cloistered environments.

I would like to give two examples from the therapies I have studied to make me a more effective counselor; the MBT-T (Mind-Body Transformation – Technique) of Drs. Ernest and Kathryn Rossi and the LifeLine Technique from Dr. Darren Weissman.

Dr. Ernest Rossi, is the heir-apparent to the late father of modern therapeutic hypnotherapy and rehabilitation, Dr. Milton Erikson, MD. With his wife, Dr. Kathryn Rossi, they have pioneered a new model of psychotherapy and life transformation that embraces the discoveries and cutting-edge knowledge around the psychobiology of gene expression called Mind-Body Transformations Therapy (MBT-T), utilizing the power and influence of verbal reflection, trance, gesture, and awareness of the subtle energy body as taught in the yoga sutras. After attending a 3-day workshop with Dr. Ernest, I undertook a private course of study with him. We looked at material of my own life that I brought to a session. Dr. Rossi then helped me explore my dreams and early morning thoughts to facilitate the growing edge of my emerging consciousness. At the end of every session, he lifted the curtain of his methods to show me what and how he did or did not do. During our sessions I seemed to discover by myself – where I have been and where I am going.

Dr. Rossi's model of the 4-Stage Creative Cycle is simple and elegant. The client presents a dilemma. The therapist helps the client understand the best of where he or she wants to go. To aid the 4-Stage Creative Cycle of uncovering positive possibilities, Dr. Rossi encourages the client to see the dilemma and the possibility of change. Through the use of mind-body language, gesture, sound, and inner vision

- all harmonized with positive intention, the client has an "AHA!" or "EUREKA!" moment and a higher order of self-awareness, integration, and awakening has taken place. Dr. Rossi explains all of this is possible because the activation of the 4-Stage Creative Cycle optimizes gene expression and brain plasticity, which is the molecular foundation for creating new consciousness and cognition to resolve problems and facilitate wellbeing.

The practice of tantra in the Buddhist tradition follows a similar pattern. For example, we want to cultivate more compassion in our lives. This is the dilemma because we do not feel that we are that compassionate to start with. Through posture (upright sitting meditation posture for the most part), gestures (hand mudras), visualizations, and mantras all focused on the aim of cultivating compassion, we are lead through the labyrinth of our own resistances to experiencing compassion in a natural manner; our self-interest, our own hatred and anger, our preferential treatment of some over others, and so forth. The tantrika – the one practicing the tantric method – is encouraged to persist in the practice and often the pain of seeing how uncompassionate and self-centered he or she is becomes glaringly obvious and painful. And then at some point, one breaks through the self-created clouds of darkness within the mind and discovers the compassionate qualities that have been there all the time.

Neuroscience of psychosocial genomics and psychoneuroimmunology can now explain what wise men and women discovered and practiced for millennia to awaken and utilize their inner resources with laser like precision. This is fantastic. But equally so is that such a forward thinking pioneer like Dr. Rossi was able to present in a modern therapeutic and scientific a seemingly simple therapeutic methods that holds similar promise for personal transformation without ecclesiastic trappings to get in the way. Dr. Rossi's integration of modern science with traditional spiritual values and holistic healing practices engage everyone to discover and utilize their inner resources for self-guidance and self-help. His theory, research and therapeutic practice is a comprehensive example of this books main theme: *The Ecology of Oneness.*

Dr. Rossi has now passed. His finally gift to me was for me to be an attendant to his process of dying. To his last breath, he demonstrated his mastery of trance. And his wife, Dr. Kathryn carries on his legacy, advancing it even further in the research the two of them shared over the decades.

Then there is the work of Dr. Darren Weissman, a chiropractor and acupuncturist who has studied with some of the great progressive minds of the 21st century; Louise Hay, Candice Pert, Dr. Masaru Emoto, Bruce Lipton, and Gregg Braden to create a methodology for quickly moving on and transforming subconscious patterning so that we can live more productive, conscious lives. This he does with what he calls the LifeLine Technique. Building upon the ancient wisdom of the subtle body energetic flows of the acupuncture meridians and the channels of the chakra grid, he uses the modern day discoveries in neuroscience and genetics, and energetic and mind transforming techniques of a variety of therapies (NLP, acupuncture, applied kinesiology, reiki, yoga, etc.). The goal of the LifeLine

Technique is for each of us to discover our own innate power, the healing power of self-love, and to live a life based upon Infinite Love and Gratitude. To my mind, the LifeLine Technique is science-based spirituality. As such, there is no immediate end to the technique as a therapy. Rather, it is a tool to facilitate the process of discovering the many levels of our existence in an open ended, loving manner. And similar to Dr. Rossi's 4-Stage Creative Cycle, the LifeLine Technique follows in an orderly fashion the sequencing of intuited esoteric wisdom and its methods that ascetics, yogis, and others committed to transformation have used over the centuries.

In both the LifeLine Technique and the 4-Stage Creative Cycle of Dr. Rossi, no archetype is called or visualized. Rather, we are using the content and context of our own lives. One is being taught or encouraged to reveal oneself to oneself: to discover that we are enough just as we are.

Will such scientifically based spiritual processes emerge as global phenomena, usurping or standing along side the roles of the traditions that have come down through the ages? Perhaps – and especially for those who at this time have been so turned off by conventional religious spirituality that they are not even attempting to search for the esoteric wisdom, obliterated or clouded over by exoteric demands. In the early days of his time in America, the Tibetan Buddhist master, Chogyam Trungpa Rinpoche said that there was much in common between Buddhist practices and modern psychotherapy. The groundbreaking work of Drs. Weissman and the Rossis extend beyond the strictly psychological and emotional dimensions of psychology to the brain plasticity and alteration of genetics that is so vital for us to grasp the more fundamental questions of our existence, access the potentials lying beneath our skin and within our hearts, leading each of us to a greater sense of holism with all that is. These discoveries and methodologies bring science into play as a support for the Ecology of Oneness perspective.

But, these are early days. My sense is that these methodologies and the ones to be spawned from them are part of the evolution of human consciousness. Thus whereas the tantric and esoteric traditions have been tested and proven over time to verify their transformational capabilities, the science that now explains, verifies, and can simulate so many aspects of such practices, has not been.

That science is verifying esoteric spiritual truths is good news for even the more conventional religious paths. Hymn singing, hand clapping, prayer gestures, and praying to whoever for whatever utilize the tools of our bodies and minds for their more noble of purposes. Furthermore, the knowledge gleaned from scientific enquiry is wearing off on these faiths as they realize that being more open minded to discoveries of the physical universe and its mysteries as seen through the telescopic and microscopic lens of science coupled with the need to be more inclusive and accepting of others paths is the only path for being able to survive and stay relevant in the free world of today. Thus, new Christian thought and the appearance of western educated students and teachers practicing Eastern paths see the relevance and necessity to bring their wisdom and too-oft concealed esoteric teachings forward in time, wedding them to quantum physics, neuroscience, and the latest discoveries in biology and other sciences. It is exciting times!

But, I am guardedly optimistic about all of this for, despite being in need of a sense of path to awaken and thus be more truly happy in life, there are so many living in a stupor of mesmerizing materialism and/or alienation who either have little interest in or have been so turned off by religions and the spirituality that so many see as synonymous with religion. In this regard, the baby has been thrown out with the bathwater. And the road to recovering, identifying with, and actually committing oneself to engage in a deeper, more fulfilling and integrated life – a life in The Ecology of Oneness – may not arise from within without more trials and tribulations.

Despite where we sometimes lead or allow ourselves to be lead, I stand firm in asserting that we all know what makes us happy. And, we all know what causes us to suffer. We all – in truth – know what is going on. We just collude with each other not to blow each other's cover or speak the truths that are staring us in the face.

That we know all of this is good. That we do little or nothing about it is a problem. But, that we know and the fact that what we know can never truly be lost means that anything is possible. Mindfulness, rooted in the intention to do good can always be summoned. And the mind technologies to take advantage of our potentials – hidden and jealously guarded by traditions in the past - are now more available than they ever have been.

Can we take advantage of the amazing possibilities for awakening in our Free World?

Chapter Eight

The Four Choices of Our Future

Nearly forty years ago, I attended a lecture given by a Tibetan Buddhist teacher by the name of Namgyal Rinpoche. Take as fact or fiction, he had come from a long family heritage of Presbyterian ministers. He, himself, was a Presbyterian minister. Then, one day, according to one of his students, he had a numinous experience where he could understand Sanskrit and felt that somehow he had other incarnations in the Far East.

All this being slightly out of his Canadian Presbyterian box, he went to the East, to a monastery called Rumtek in Gangtok, Sikkim, where he sought some answers from one of Tibet's great yogis of the twentieth century, The Sixteenth Gyalwa Karmapa. The Karmapas are said to know the past, present, and future; hence also known as "Knower of the Three Times."

The white, Presbyterian minister went in front of the Karmapa, whose first words to him were, something to the effect of "You're back!" to which the minister said, "What do you mean I'm back?" The Karmapa then told him that he was Namgyal Rinpoche, a wrathful emanation of the great saint, Padmasambhava. And, somehow, it all then made sense.

While you are digesting all this, I invite you to read on...

I only saw Namgyal Rinpoche once. London, 1976. Among the many pearls of wisdom he spoke that day was a vision of the future. It was not a rosy, utopian vision. Rather, he saw a time of darkness where the majority of the human population was going through very difficult, harsh times. Governments would be draconian in their responses. Mediocrity in the form of over-bureaucratization would reign and most people who feel suppressed and conflicts would be frequent. In my book, *Wisdom of the Buddhist Masters*, I interviewed a number of other Buddhist teachers about the next fifty to one hundred years. Whilst most of the Western Buddhist teachers show some signs of optimism, the Tibetan teachers see a similar vision to Namgyal Rinpoche. They feel that the momentum of materialism and the greed that has fostered and capitalized on it was too vast and all-pervading to turn around towards a more positive direction; that like civilizations that have come and gone, ours would continue to degrade and with that degradation, there would be more sickness, poverty, and warfare.

What is interesting is that being almost a bridge between the younger, more enthusiastic white Western teachers and the oriental Tibetan teachers is that Namgyal Rinpoche said that there would be "pockets of light" in the dark ages to come. I mention Namgyal Rinpoche and alluded to this notion in a previous chapter. These pockets of light were like-minded people with critical thinking skills, desiring to remain present and connected to their world, acting out of their desire to be the best spiritual beings having a human experience as they could be. These pocket people would preserve and pass on knowledge and methods to future generations, keeping the best of humanity alive in small communities throughout the world.

So, what does this look like?

In my mind, I witness and envision there being four possible choices in terms of who we are and how we act and move into the future we are creating. In the chaotic and challenging world I have been speaking of throughout this book, these choices are as follows.

Option One

Cover your ears, close your eyes, shut the doors, and throw out or radically censor all media that reaches your eyes and ears and the eyes and ears of your loved ones. Remain chosen and only relate to those who are chosen like yourself. If you can, stay in a compound, preferably far away from other influences; a mountain, a hidden valley, an island...

The success of this is unlikely. With space as information and change a constant, you will lose generations along the way.

Option Two

Still consider yourself as chosen, as one of a group of people like yourself who are convinced that your answer is the right answer and then banish, marginalize, convert or kill all others not yet chosen. Continue to evangelize, discredit others, assimilate them where you can, have them submit to your dominance, or kill them, keeping to policies, practices, and rationales that justify at ordinary and transcendent levels the exclusivity you seek in the world. Manifest Destiny, Jihad, ethnic cleansing – nothing is out of bounds if your vision is a sanitized, homogenized world of Chosen Ones like yourself.

The success of this actually becoming the dominant option humans chose in the world we live in is remote. But, such people can really make a mess, which is more often than not, cleaned up by others.

Option Three

Sick of the marketing and murder of chosen people fanatics, of the diddling of little boys by priests, and the perpetual guilt trips around sexuality and generally just enjoying yourself, you abandon any sense of a possible transcendent, inter-related, multi-faceted reality and the value of spiritual aspiration. In Tibetan Ayurveda, it is said that spiritual poison is the worst kind of poison. Why? Because corruption, deception, and perversion and guilt tripping in an attempt to keep members believing through fear and coercion has led to an ever increasing secular world where spirituality is decried as childish at best, disempowering and destructive of human joy, worth, dignity, even life itself. The result of this disenchantment is that ordinary human morality and decency, historically defined as or cloaked in religious terms, risks getting tossed out as irrelevant or meaningless as a cause in the betterment and upliftment between parents and children, friends, even nations. Materialism becomes god and life is thus measured in terms of acquisition and power.

Maybe you have never been poisoned by bad religion or values or mores or circumstances that have crushed your spirit. Maybe you are just a part of the happy consumer culture, waiting for the next iPod, the next social media buzz. Or maybe you just want to be left alone to live your life as the best humans you can be; a humanist if you will. But, like those who now ardently reject a more profound sense of the world and what is possible and the desire to connect with it, when crises arise and we move closer to the end of life, the larger questions about life and worlds unseen loom bigger. Stripped naked of your acquisitions, your youthfulness, or prowess and reliance on a body that inevitably crumbles for each and every one of us, without endeavoring in any meaningful, conscious, or consistent manner to reach beyond the three dimensional world, what resources do we have to embrace whatever comes next with dignity and grace?

The group of this option, the ones that want to be left alone, will be the greater number of people on the planet. But, focused on just getting by and being left alone, they will be more susceptible to the mediocrity and meaninglessness of a material reality collapsing. Without a sense of spiritual connection and having been put off by the religions they themselves rejected or the fanaticism and tyranny of those who profess spiritual sanction, their alienation will lead to greater levels of uncertainty and a need for more and more entertainment, diversion, and medication. Today, the America in which I am citizen seems somewhat confused as to whether it should celebrate or cringe with the ongoing legalization of marijuana. But as marijuana and other similar psychotropic drugs are being used more for recreation than exploration or as aids in spiritual transformation, and with the growing over-consumption of alcohol, designer drugs, and the vast array of mind-numbing pharmaceuticals, we are in the age of soma as predicted by Aldous Huxley.

"Comfortably numb" may be our desire. But the reality of such proves soul destroying.

Option Four

Developing critical thinking skills and connecting with your loving nature through intellectual inquiry, contemplation, meditation, and perhaps supported by any number of other mind-body integration practices (yoga, dance, trance work, singing, drumming, psychotherapy, the sacred use of substances, etc.) your compassion and kindness grow as you embrace that which brings out light within yourself and supports others to do the same. Despite the endlessly disempowering cultural messages that leads so many to feel isolated unless one becomes a part of the frenzy of consumption, you awaken to a world that you are a part of and never really been separate from. With discriminating awareness, less and less swayed by negative emotions, self-doubt, and fear, you look at all dimensions of what we as humans have created, take note of what is most useful to apply and what no longer works or applies to your circumstance, and work with others to construct a local, sustainable community to foster awakening individuation and supporting and protecting the needs of others to attain such.

In the Ecology of Oneness, you develop a deep understanding and appreciation that you do not have to be the same as or in lockstep with the various others with whom you share your vision, but rather that each contributes consciously and compassionately to the Whole in the best possible way they know how, individually and collectively.

And, with a spirit of inclusivity, as the people of options one, two, and three find greater disillusion, you embrace and support them in their process of awakening.

Of course, you still may have a utopian starry-eyed hope and wish that all of society wakes up and gets transformed to be an inclusive, sustainable, ecological paradise; that an Ecology of Oneness permeates and transforms every level of society, eradicating sickness, poverty, and warfare forever. Who would not want such an existence? Yet, other than the skepticism voiced by Eastern teachers on this matter, I am again reminded of the lesson I learned in the late 1970's from another Tibetan teacher at a retreat center in upstate New York, that I shared at the very beginning of this book.

His words seemed harsh, but their truth has proven itself time and again in my life and in many who I have counseled and broken bread with over the years. "If you embrace the Dharma (actually meaning the way things are and making efforts to wake up to it – parentheses my own), you will be treated lower than a dog in the street." "Conventional wisdom" of any time does not like to be shown up. Even if people are wallowing in misery, the habit of being in such only elicits fear or disdain when options of other possibilities are offered. That is, until the pain of being stuck or in denial far outstrips the power of the habit to remain in that place. Until that time, don't expect to be liked for what you offer. And even then, even if what you reveal or offer is accepted, don't expect thanks. A courageous and altruistic heart is needed here.

When I take the caveats of all these learned teachers together and then reference the world that I witness around me and see through various forms of media, my personal conclusion is to side with the "pockets of light" thesis; that is, I do not see for the foreseeable future a world embracing organic, natural, inclusive, sustainable approaches. Greed is sill too strong. Absolutes still intoxicate a good number. And alcohol and pharmaceuticals keep everyone else dozing at the wheel of a world once again teetering towards another human civilization dying off. The 2020-2021 global response to the Covid 19 pandemic has demonstrated that greed is still in the driver's seat, running ramshackle over disadvantaged people, communities, and nations. This response will have long-term adverse effects in all segments of living, everywhere. Whoever is to survive in these times, it is my hope that they find communities of light, ready to offer what has been cherished and held to re-seed what we can all hope will be the society we wish would happen now.

I do not believe in an apocalypse where all human life dies or the world incinerates in a ball of nuclear fire. Because I believe that basic goodness is the core aspect of who we are fundamentally, as the world around us deteriorates, I see this innate quality surfacing and becoming more of a guiding light. In that regard, I think that the ranks within these pockets of light will grow, though never to become the dominant paradigm. Within communities around the world, these pockets will appear in a number of guises; as growth centers of various kinds, yoga studios, meditation centers, study groups, communal living experiments, virtual collectives, dinner parties, virtual networks forged during the pandemic, maybe even as businesses, political parties, and various other inventive ways that people of an

Ecology of Oneness mind may come to gather. As refuges and wells from which those who are hungry and thirsty will drink, my hope is these pockets of light inspire a gradual awakening to slow and reverse the ravages of our materialist march in these times.

I am not holding out for a totally transformed world – nor do I think this really matters. In the Shambhalian tradition of the East, it is said that our planet is a training ground and place to be tested. If there is, therefore, a heaven to be or a heaven that awaits us, maybe it is not nor never will be here. Maybe utopia lies somewhere else. But, if the name of the game is to awaken, perhaps once peace and openness reigns between our ears and in our hearts, the pursuit for that land will be less important as we do the work of helping ourselves and others along.

We are all in this together; always were, always will be. And each of us has to grow through stages of awareness to get to an acceptance and enjoyment of this fact. At times we may feel cut off from anything spiritual within us. Other times, we feel stirrings and assume that it is because of the time, the circumstance, the people we are with, God's, the guru's or Jesus' blessing. If deeper inquiry leads us to realize that all of the good feelings arise from within us, we may pull back, maybe even think that we can do it all – grow-up to finally be the spiritual beings having a human experience we have always been. But, the simple fact is that the only way we can know, the only way this can be tested is in relationship. In how others respond to us and what emotions arise in our interactions with them, we get a true sense of how far we have progressed along the way. We need each other as mentors, friends, supports, mirrors in order to grow and thrive individually and collectively.

There is work to be done. And it is best done with friends and others with whom we feel a kinship and sense of purpose. This is a time to reach out, find those who seek or exude light in your community, allow your basic goodness and the love that flows from it grow, and cherish each and every moment we have. Of all the knowledge of what it will take to rebuild from the madness and ashes of these material times, if we remember these things alone, whatever flows from them will be the best possible foundation upon which to build – or perhaps continue and expand a more sustainable, loving, thriving, amazing planet.

Perhaps there are always individuals within each generation who feel that as they are coming to the end of their mortal days, that the planet or society or civilization is in peril – simply because they themselves are close to death. However, judging by Lemuria, Atlantis, Rome, and the many other civilizations and empires that have come and gone, perhaps the caveats from those who may have been called any number of names - nay-sayers, sooth-sayers, crackpots, madmen, or prophets - are not without merit. And the harbingers of the times we are in are well worth heeding.

I contend that no good thought is ever wasted and the goodness that comes from such can be built upon and expand. Thus, whilst I am saddened to see so many suffer as they do in these days and despite the fact that I feel that more suffering is to come, if I recoil, reject, or turn away from those around me, I do nothing to create a bridge to something better.

So, for me, I chose Option Four. I embrace an Ecology of Oneness in my desire to awaken in a Free World.

I wouldn't know what else to do.

Chapter Nine

Closing Remarks and

The Only Belief Almost Worth Having

What are the lessons and messages I want you to take away from this book?

In telling my own personal story and journey towards an awareness and embracing on an Ecology of Oneness, I wanted to stir in you an awareness that you are not alone and that whatever straight and narrow or circuitous path you have taken to come to a similar position in your life is valid and essential in these times. As I mentioned in the previous chapter, we do not have to be in lockstep, all drinking the same Kool-Aid, for us to learn the lessons we need to absorb and turn into the action steps to create or hold as a promise an inclusive, sustainable, peaceful, thriving world.

I then wanted to share with you some of the useful musings and steps I have taken to fortify my resolve in this vision. Of utmost importance is an appreciation and respect for impermanence – one of the most vital understandings we can have if we want to walk a path of humility and gratitude. The vastness of our universe, the ever-changing nature of our bodies, the evolutions and revolutions of mind and consciousness in the mix of humans in all possible circumstances brings us to an awareness as to what is absolutely true and what is relatively useful.

I wanted you to fully understand that what you think and how you act *does* matter. To make this crystal clear, I explained karma, reincarnation and things related to these notions in order for you to grasp that, in truth, we are all in this for the long haul; that as fractals of God, the Hound of Heaven is going to stay on our heels until we wake up in the grace, light, and love of who we are in this amazing universe. In this process of waking up to who we are, we do need friends, helpers, transcendent and invisible beings with whom to cooperate and interact with to get the job done – for ourselves individually, and collectively.

And, finally, that we are in the time of choosing. How do we want to step forward in our lives? How do we want to overcome the sickness, poverty, warfare, and greed in the world, the reality of which we buy into and, as a result, find ourselves feeling at times disconnected, dis-empowered, and desperate? The job to truly overcome such feelings is the inner process of awakening as I have lain out. And the benefits of such are reflected in the world around us and how people respond to our words and deeds. But, I caution everyone not to believe that such transformation and the coming together into "pockets of light" communities that I outline will see the end of the pain and suffering that is so pervasive in our world. As this world of ours is a laboratory of transformation, I concur with many teachers with who I have studied, that we are still in for dark times. Like a disease process and the path of recovery, there are fevers and discharges, and pains along the way. In this current cycle of time, it is hard to determine how far down the road to recovery we are. At times, it feels like not so far. Environmental degradation, new and more insidious pandemics, and the collapse of nations, societies, and cultures will continue as the Three Poisons of ignorance, attachment, and aggression are being transformed. People will suffer. Some will awaken in this life. Others will not. We need to be kind, compassionate, strong, and resolute. There is still much to be done and great value in staying true to The Ecology of Oneness. And, there are generations to come. We owe it to them to be mentors and friends to support them in their own processes of awakening and carrying The Ecology of Oneness banner forward.

To be engaged in such a noble task as a "spiritual being having a human experience," one may presume that part of this courage and resolve is to believe in oneself. So often, human potential pundits encourage such. There is value in this to a point. But, I would like to add some final words for you to go beyond even this. To do so, like so many times in this book, I shall start with the part of my own journey that is most appropriate to illustrate.

On June 11th, 2014 my beloved teacher, Kunzig Shamar Rinpoche suddenly died. He has been the most significant teacher of mine for the last twenty years of the 33 years that we have known each other. In the backyard of a friend's house in the beginning of our relationship years, he gave me instructions on seeing directly the nature of my mind. And over the years this has proven itself to be the most important teaching of my life. I am sad to see him go, but also know that great Bodhisattvas have control over such matters and use even their dying as a teaching to expand our awareness and growth.

At the time Shamar Rinpoche "burned my boat," after he told me that we should never meet again, his last instruction to me was that I should serve no other Tibetan lama. As I said in the Dedication, I did not take this event as a tragic end to our long relationship, but rather a new episode. Rinpoche had told me that my sangha, my community, was the people I wrote for. Considering how troublesome I was in Tibetan Buddhist groups, I knew at once the significance of this message. For me, as I have also written in this book, my sangha is larger than just those associated with Tibetan teachers or Buddhism for that matter. And, it seems almost prophetic that the completion of this manuscript about the necessity of an inclusive state of mind for the growth and development of a community rooted in the Ecology of Oneness has come since the time of his passing. Thus not only is this book dedicated to Rinpoche, I also offer it up to him in appreciation and to all of you as the best offering I can make at this time for the spawning and spreading of Pockets of Light.

And so, as a final thought to this book I would like to express the following.

There is only one belief to almost have: belief in oneself. All beliefs that you hold about the world, about God, and so forth will eventually lead you astray. That is why I say "almost believing" in oneself, for even holding onto this belief is precarious. It should be held ever so lightly.

Until the illusion of separation is transcended and you are living in the full light of Oneness, fixation on your life as being this or that, of who or what you think you are will eventually unravel and lead to disappointment. Like tethers to hold a boat from capsizing in rough waters, once the seas subside, you need to untether your boat to get on with the journey. Whatever you hold too tightly as true or believe about yourself, you are more than that. All that is awake, all the potentials you need to radiate that awakened state is already within you. You are complete.

In fact, in the spirit of distinguishing belief as dogma that may or may not have limited benefits from faith as something worth testing, have confidence in yourself and *faith* that by listening to the wisdom of your inherent awakening potential – your Buddhanature – that – in a world that you know now you are inseparable from - you will move forward, assess, adjust, and find those in your life – the pocket of light community - you are resonant with. Wherever you are in your process and journey, you use it as a springboard from which to stretch even further. Beliefs have limits. Faith is open ended.

What that means ultimately is that in and for the long run, don't believe in or hold onto solid beliefs in anything. We do need grounding and stability, but if we clutch to tight too what we think we need to do this, things come undone and we shall inevitably wind up in shaky territory. So, pay attention. See if what you hold to fits and works here and now. As we are actually smarter than we think, project yourself down the road. Reflect again.

Put yourself out into the world. Do it in a way that feels natural to you. If you are more of an introvert or introspective person, be wary of shrinking away. Be particularly watchful against self-denigration. Putting yourself down is the worst of all possible sins. If you are more outwardly focused, you may get arrogant and cocky. Chances are, the world will speak to you and let you know that you have exceeded your limits.

As you discover more and more the truth of who you are, you will grow beyond measure in a balanced, healthy, and loving way. The Ecology of Oneness is not about reckless abandon. Hedonism or Bohemianism is self-serving and unsustainable. Such approaches are just ego-based rationalizations for doing what you want to do without real regard for others. But at the same time, cowering inside yourself is also ego-based as it sucks others into the vortex of you viewing your life as a problem. Avoid these extremes.

In the world we are living in today, in the world we want to build and sustain for future generations, the Ecology of Oneness relies on those who confidently love themselves and can reach from the deep well of that self-love to include others in a loving embrace. And we all know that this is a magnificent feedback loop.

In that mythical and transformational time of the 1960's, the Beatles came around just to remind us that, "All you need is love." Simple and deep.

In this, there is nothing to believe. In our bones, we know this as truth. Our job – the fruition of who we are as spiritual beings - is to have faith in our loving nature, then live it, test it, grow it, and share it.

Above all, share it.

In the spirit of The Ecology of Oneness and Awakening in a Free World,

Robert

A Helpful Bibliography

Here are some of my books and the books of others that I hope will be of use and worthy of your consideration...

Gregory, Jason. *The Science and Practice of Humility: The Path to Ultimate Freedom.* Rochester, Vermont, Toronto: Inner Traditions, 2014.

Hayward, Jeremy. *Sacred World: A Guide to Shambhala Warriorship in Daily Life.* New York, Toronto, London, Sydney, Auckland: Bantam Books, 1995.

Freke, Tim. *The Mystery Experience: A Revolutionary Approach to Spiritual Awakening.* London: Watkins Publishing, 2012.

Kornfield, Jack. *The Wise Heart: A Guide to the Universal Teachings of Buddhist Psychology.* New York: Bantam Books, 2008.

Kunzig Shamar Rinpoche. (Edited by Lara Braitstein) *The Path To Awakening.* Delhi: Motilal Banarsidass Publishers, 2009

Levine, Stephen. *Turning Towards the Mystery.* New York: Harper Collins. 2002

Nydahl, Lama Ole. *Fearless Death: Buddhist Wisdom on the Art of Dying.* Darmstadt, Diamond Way Press, 2012.

Rossi, Dr. Ernest. *Creating Consciousness: How Therapists Can Facilitate Wonder, Wisdom, Truth, and Beauty.* Phoenix, AZ: Milton H. Erikson Foundation Press, 2012.

Sachs, Robert. *The Passionate Buddha: Wisdom on Intimacy and Enduring Love.* Rochester, VT: Inner Traditions, 2002

Sachs, Robert. *Becoming Buddha: Awakening the Wisdom and Compassion to Change Your World.* London: Watkins Publishing, 2010.

Sachs, Robert. *The Wisdom of The Buddhist Masters: Common and Uncommon Sense.* London: Watkins Publishing, 2008.

Sachs, Robert. *Rebirth into Pure Land: A True Story of Birth, Death, and Transformation and How We Can Prepare for The Most Amazing Journey of Our Lives.* San Luis Obispo: Robert Sachs (via CreateSpace), 2012.

Sri Nisargadatta Maharaj. (translated buy Maurice Frydman) *I Am That.* Durham, NC: The Acorn Press, 1973.

Trungpa, Ven. Chogyam. *Shambhala: The Sacred Path of The Warrior.* Boulder and London: Shambhala, 1984.

Walsh, James and Tugwell, Simon (editors). *The Cloud of Unknowing.* New york, Ramsey, Toronto: Paulist Press, 1981.

Weissman, Dr. Darren. *The Power of Infinite Love and Gratitude: An Evolutionary Journey to Awakening Your Spirit.* Carlsbad, New York City, London, Sydney, Johannesburg, Vancouver, Hong Kong, New Delhi: Hay House, Inc., 2005.

Yassami, Hoja Ahmed. (translated by Jonathan and Virve Trapman) *Divine Wisdom: Diwani Hikmet.* Glastonbury: Living Zen Books, 2013.

Yogananda, Paramahansa. *Autobiography of a Yogi.* Los Angeles: Self-Realization Fellowship, 1946.

About the Author

Robert Sachs has been engaged in an integrated approach to health and spirituality for over forty years, being educated in both Western and Eastern philosophy, spirituality, psychology and healthcare. He holds a B.A. in Comparative Religion and Sociology, a Masters in Social Work, and has a practice as a clinical social worker and Certified LifeLine Practitioner. Along with his conventional training and vocations, Robert has been the student of some the world's great eastern spiritual teachers and healers since 1973. He has been a certified yoga and meditation teacher since 1976, a licensed massage therapist for over thirty years, is recognized as a master and instructor of Tibetan and Indian Ayurvedic bodywork, and author of hundreds of articles found in health and spiritual magazines and 7 books on Buddhist philosophy and practice and various aspects of holistic health care, including

- *Nine Star Ki: Feng Shui Astrology for Deepening Self-Knowledge and Enhancing Relationships, Health, and Prosperity*
- *Tibetan Ayurveda: Health Secrets from The Roof of The World*
- *Perfect Endings: A Conscious Approach to Dying and Death*
- *Rebirth Into Pure Land: A True Story of Birth, Death, and Transformation and How We Can Prepare for The Most Amazing Journey of Our Lives*
- *The Passionate Buddha: Wisdom on Intimacy and Enduring Love*
- *Becoming Buddha: Awakening the Wisdom and Compassion to Change Your World*
- *The Wisdom of The Buddhist Masters: Common and Uncommon Sense*
- *Start Your Day with a Good Night's Sleep*
- *Psychic Whackos Save America – a True Story*
- *The Path of Civility: Perfecting the Lessons of a President by Applying the Wisdom of a Buddha*

Robert lives in Oceano, California on an urban farm with his wife, Melanie, where they run Diamond Way Ayurveda. Their son, Jabeth and his Beloved, Kinsey. homestead in their tiny house on the farm.